The Unwanted Child

A JOURNEY FROM REJECTION TO REDEMPTION

DR. FRANTZ LAMOUR

The Unwanted child: A Journey from Rejection to Redemption
Copyright 2024— Dr. Frantz Lamour
All rights reserved. The use of short quotations for personal or group study is encouraged. No portion of this book may be copied or reproduced for commercial gain.
Frantz Lamour Ministries, Inc.
2145 S Military Trail
West Palm Beach, FL 33415
ISBN: 979-8-9909833-3-5
Printed in the U.S.A.
For more information on distributions, call (561) 827-2760
Or reach us at drfrantzlamour@gmail.com

DEDICATION

To my mother, whose courage and resilience gave me life and purpose.

To my wife, whose love and unwavering support strengthen me every day.

To my family, whose presence and encouragement fuel my journey.

This book is for you, my greatest inspiration and the foundation of all I strive to be.

CONTENTS

Introduction 7

Chapter 1: Heaven's Design – Where I Came From 9

Chapter 2: A Dark Beginning – Born into Rejection 15

Chapter 3: An Unlikely Protector – The Strength of My Mother's Love 27

Chapter 4: Growing in Absence – A Childhood Without a Father 35

Chapter 5: Lost and Searching – Struggling to Find My Way . 49

Chapter 6: A Divine Intervention: Finding Jesus in 1986 57

Chapter 7: The Meeting That Changed Everything – Encountering My Father 63

Chapter 8: Forged in Faith: The Discipline of God's Word 73

Chapter 9: A Vision for Love: Embracing God's Purpose 83

Chapter 10: A Husband and Father—Learning to Love and Lead 97

Chapter 11: A Call to Lead: Founding the Love Kingdom 115

Chapter 12: From Counselor to Creator: A Journey of Talents 123

Chapter 13: Legacy and Love: Building a Lasting Impact 131

Chapter 14: Your Story Matters: Embracing God's Purpose in You 139

Final Words 145

INTRODUCTION

You never know where the inspiration will come from or what moment will push you to discover and embrace your talents. This book was birthed during a conversation with an 11-year-old 5th grader named Siannah S., whose mother graciously permitted her to share her name. We discussed self-worth, childhood, and aspirations when the topic shifted to the people who shaped us—those who were present and those who were absent. After hearing about my upbringing, my journey, and the accomplishments I have achieved, this young girl looked at me and said, "Wow, you have an incredible story. You should write a book about your life." I listened to her words and took them to heart. And so, here we are—this book is the result.

In this book, I hope that through my story, you will wish to explore, evolve, and unleash your inner self. Your creative side will give birth to inventions that add value to humanity. Each great accomplishment begins with an equally great inspiration, and I am thankful to my fifth-grade student for sharing my story with the world.

What you will read in *The Unwanted Child* is a story of metamorphosis—a testimony of God's love, faith, and the great purpose He has for every person. It is a story of hope that brings perspective to our journeys—it is a reminder that our identity is never determined by our situation, our suffering, or what society seeks to tag us with. In God's eyes, we are all of value and distinct for a reason: We have a purpose that He has carefully designed for us.

That is not just a tale of struggling through oppression to become a winner; it is a story of a reason to live, determination, and God's unshakable love. From a young Haitian boy who faced challenges and rejection, I somehow fueled my faith and became a leader and a man of God. My story carries with it a simple yet profound truth: no matter how difficult our beginnings may be, they cannot diminish the incredible plans God has for us.

My name is Frantz Lamour, and I entered this world without a father's support. Thank you, Mother, for making the tough decision of giving me life, however rough it may have been or instead even going to be. What has followed has been a lifetime of pain, disappointment, and the profound realization of the love of God and the meaning of life. This book invites you to join me in that journey, hoping to inspire you to trust God's plan for your life, even when the road ahead is blurred.

CHAPTER 1:

Heaven's Design - Where I Came From

I was raised where the mountains touched the sky and the oceans whispered sweet songs with the waves—such is the power of creation's rhythm. I am talking about Haiti—a country deeply rooted in culture, filled with beauty and resilience that best describes the people's hearts. Haiti has always appeared to me as more than a place to be born. The earth nurtured my beginning, a land interlaced with love, pain, and meaning.

Growing up, I never fully understood the concept of "purpose." It was a word often spoken by teachers and pastors, who would urge us to discover ours. However, through that scope, life appeared a blurry haze; the future a blur, let alone purpose that only those poised among us seemed to possess. In those days, even while I battled through difficulties, Haiti had started to narrate the corners of my purpose, a logic dominated by the land, people, and God's overwhelming cosmic intent.

As I have discovered over time, there are many things I have learned from Haiti—for example, the importance of determination and hard work. Although we lived in a more modest household, my family always made do. After all, why wait for help when you can find solutions to obstacles as they arise? For example, when storms hit, we thrived rather than waiting for aid. Even in dry seasons, when the heat would crack the land, my grandmother would tell us, "Haiti is made of fierce people who fight till the end." At a young age, I was exposed to the notion that beauty can stem from places of pain, and no matter how ugly the circumstances we find ourselves in, they do not dictate who we are. That knowledge was invaluable.

Fast forwarding to the modern day, it is apparent today that God has accompanied me in every single part of my life, even when walking to school on those humble roads. However, that humble journey was far more than a mere walk. As a kid, I was blind to my surroundings, which gave me little to no purpose, but now, looking back at it, I realize those roads were crucial to my development. Patience, humility, perseverance— all great reminders of where I came from. I had no idea these qualities would later help me go through life as a Counselor, a Leader, and a Servant to others.

Mirroring the image of God in Day-To-Day Activities

Of several memories of my mother, I specifically remember how she used to take the single most simplistic ingredients to prepare a meal. She made the most out of what was available, making what seemed ordinary the answer to the unending question of hunger. Watching her, I understood that God's design is often about taking what we are given, no matter how little or humble, and finding a way to use it purposefully. She showed me that purpose was not about having the most or doing the most significant things but faithfulness in what we have.

We had something remarkable in our hearts in Haiti; it was God's image. The older church people would always explain, 'N'ap viv pou Bondye,' meaning 'We live for God.' When my grandma held close her little ones, I could tell it meant much more than those nameless words of protection. I saw others around our houses using hand pumps to fetch water or exchange vegetables from their backyard gardens. We had faith that everyone had a portion of God that needed shelter, care, and protection to be nurtured into doing good.

The Strength of Purpose in Adversity

Life has certainly been challenging in Haiti. At times, I felt the hardships to be insurmountable. I found purpose in this inner voice, which unifies with God's essence, especially in challenging times. It taught me that God loves us all unceasingly and always gives us the strength to embrace difficulties.

It could have been many years ago when a man stood up to speak in church after a storm destroyed many homes in our village. The man had lost almost everything, but he said, "Nou kabab toujou fè limyè klere." That means in English, "We can always let the light shine." Because of all the storms, his house was turned into a ruin, as were his fields, but he still believed in something more significant than the storms: *hope*. That was the strength and faith I carried whenever I set foot in Haiti. It was the kind of strength I would have with me in all the future challenges that awaited me.

My memory today reminds me that I was created for something much bigger. Everything Haiti emphasizes was a planting ground for me to nurture a desire to serve, lead, and instill hope in others. Having been born in a place where I could not find many options available, I grasped that we as people had much more than this: the belief that all of us were a lot stronger and greater than mere surplus counts. All of us have been created in God's image, allowing us to do something our situation may imply otherwise.

It is comforting to know that some aspects of our lives have meaning. I can personally attest to this by observing how people begin to appreciate themselves after participating in Counseling sessions. I also find this sense of purpose among the youths I minister to as they search for self-help and self-discovery. It is right there in my kids' eyes as I impress them that God also created them for a reason and a calling.

Looking back at my beginnings, along with the proverbial words of the music, has led me to appreciate how Heaven's Blueprint works, how it has relevance in everyone's life, and how it is not something that is bestowed upon the Chosen Ones alone. That purpose is the strength instilled in us through the good and troubled times and all our endeavors. It calls out to us softly during the calm and turbulence as a reminder that there was great intent in the creation of man to fulfill goals and to lead a life in reverence to God.

I hail from this, and I was impressed in many ways. The reality within us all is the work of God's design. I may have come from Haiti, but even if this place is long forgotten, its teachings of faith, resilience, and sense of purpose are everlasting, just the way God wanted it to be. I am imbued with Heaven's design, and through my story, I wish that the desire also possesses you.

CHAPTER 2:

A Dark Beginning - Born into Rejection

My Story Begins with My Brave Mom

My story began long before I entered the world stage. Although this may sound paradoxical, I am painting a picture of utter chaos here. Beginning with my mother's life has been laced with suffering, pain, and denial, but at the same time, much bravery. So, it was her courage that allowed us both to pull through those times. So, to some extent, her story becomes part of mine, and her strength and faith through the hardest of times is something I had the making to understand even before I could even spell faith.

My mom's early life was in Haiti, where she was 15 years old and lived with her aunt. One day, she got invited by her aunt's friend, and like any other girl's young mother would, there was no second thought. She was a young and innocent child woman wounded by an older man who exploited her condition. That rendered her perplexed, terrified, embarrassed, and anxious about whom to confide in.

There was a time in our culture when giving birth without being married was seen as bringing shame to the family, not only the girl but more so her mother. Everyone was aware that the mother would be in for some harsh words. It's all in the family. She also explored all the potential ramifications, including getting rid of it and not giving birth.

As we delve into the deepest recesses of her head, there comes a moment when she can be heard whispering to herself: "What do we know of what this child will turn out to be? I am going to have my child." It is an unforgivable offense in the eyes of society. She does not care and decides to go ahead with it, all while raising me the same way as her child, and eventually, her decision changed the outlook for both of us. She made clear that it does not matter how dark the situation is; there is always a positive aspect somewhere waiting to be found.

I had to face all that, but I said, 'The more I suffered, the better the person I became.' That was something I learned from my mother. The urge to live my mother's dream was so strong that nothing could have been an obstacle for me—nothing ever could.

A Mother's Heart Amidst Shame and Sacrifice

On a lighter note, my mother suffered even more due to one of her older sisters because she was the epitome of disbelief and tongue-lashing when my mother disclosed her pregnancy. Instead of answering in pride and expecting an encouraging response, her sister slapped and scolded her. Such a refusal was a brutal betrayal for her, as she felt an unfulfilled expectation, and so she was forced to withdraw from those who should have served as the object of her pity.

In a symbolic act of self-projection, my mother tried to partially disassociate herself from her sister's family by choosing another last name. Eventually, she also adopted her grandfather's first name, *Lamour*, which means Love in English, which was, in a way, not losing her sense of purpose and, more importantly, her sense of self for the pain.

However, as I could not assume the surname of my biological father, my mother went ahead to create a name for me, which was one in which life was to love God and people. Was this something that just happened by chance? I do not think so. Even in such a moment when my mother, for instance, did not yet know God personally, I now understand the playing of God in the back. That name today indicates how God wants me to put His love across a world of sorrows. For this, I thank you endlessly.

Furthermore, my mother gave me the name "Frantz," a German name that means 'a free man.' As it turns out, this name has also become part of the story of my life. It is astonishing how perfectly this name correlates with the direction God had in mind for me – nature and love-stirring, without fail and captivating with belief. That is nothing short of miraculous – a glorious evidence of the effect that God's power can have. Alas, there is no chance my mother could grasp the comprehensiveness of the picture that God was knitting at that time. Yet, in despair, rejection, and grief, she made those choices and developed a sophisticated plan.

Thank you, Mother. You are my hero, a woman who faced tribulations, conquered every bit of life's challenges, and gave me a heritage enriched with power and will to succeed. Naturally, I do not remember those few first seconds, but I know the tale well enough, having heard it so many times that it is nearly inked in me.

My mother told me things like this - "As a young woman, I should not have to choose whether to keep a raped child which the society was ready to take up or abandon it" The society called her to get rid of the shame differently. But she gave me love that covers her with shame, brings me alive, and also allows me to flourish by nourishing me in her womb.

My mother never had a good relationship with her father, who was a voodoo priest, something that she had resented since childhood. She did not believe in his faith or practices as magic, and these beliefs amounted to barriers to trust. A father brought her up as a voodoo priest's daughter ought to, which is to accept the spiritual norms that had governed unquestioningly and, at times, imprisoned his life. These fragmented relationships only heightened her benign feeling of isolation. She would reach out to him in the weakest moments of her life, only to be deserted because her betrayal of his ways was too much for him to fathom.

Also, there was some void of forgotten struggles that existed in my mother that could never disappear, which would always provide my mother with the power to state without any qualms that there is someone in disguise who has a higher power who is a Creator, other than what her father practiced.

She found peace in the idea that a God created her and governs the world, even if she cannot communicate with him. Such muted aspirations gave her a perspective and a sense of polestar to shape values, giving her the strength to endure pain. Although it was not accurately put, the idea of God and the powerful impression of Him instilled in her a hope that she would be able to do something different, which, the time would show, the actual destination towards the Real Source of Love and Grace.

Standing Pace also remembers the unbearable pain during those times of agitation she recalls. During the times of restlessness, she remembers nights like the one where she spent hours gripped in the fetal position and self-hugging, praying to a nonspecific 'God' she had never encountered, begging for help and strength when she was unsure whether the actions she undertook were even correct. People who escaped a repetitive disinterest that followed after a feeling of limitless love would hold her and explain it as one of the reasons why she felt God or God's pushing hand or a dignified kiss as the assurances.

My mother could see but could not tell the world her child had sense, which caused her to ignore the condescending voices at the corners, forcing her to push forth and instill in her child the belief that her hope was far from finding approval on a superficial level. At least when the world has told a different story, I have to say that my first name, as it was given to me, is packed with meaning and provides an opportunity to recall the purpose of God's sacrifice and his plan for my life.

Sharing the Experience of Being 'Not Good Enough'

I remember my mother and I forming a formidable bond ever since childhood. At that time, she was struggling to find a job and was not getting any help or assistance from the people in her surroundings. Some days were terrible, and life could be described as one filled with suffering, often hunger struck, and we could barely think of when we would have our next meal. But she scornfully decided and resolved not to nurture any feelings of bitterness or resentment. She insisted we are more than what our circumstances dictate and, regardless of the countless times that people would disparage us, we can hold our heads high with dignity and faith. However, she was heartbroken, and her heart was big, and she said God would take care of us. Her words composed my songs while her thoughts spoke through me.

I remember one time when I was about five. My mom had taken me to a small supermarket, and when she was about to pay, I noticed how people looked at my mom - they were talking in whispers, staring sideways or straight at her as if she were *'A lady with an unwanted child.'* I was just a little kid, so I could not understand much, but I felt the weight of their harsh thoughts. Please do not get me wrong; she bore all the stares she received, and having cast a glance at them, she went away with me in their glaring sight. All my life, I have lived in my imagination, relying on other perspectives rather than God, violating his purpose.

A Struggle Helped by Faith

The heroin was selected without the bottle being opened. Some days, my mother would sit in a corner, crying silently, while I would approach her, trying to find out what happened. As she wiped off her tears with a smile, she would pat me on my shoulder and exclaim, "Frantz, you are my delight." I remember her saying that even though she was unaware of God, he was present for us. She ensured that we pulled through if there were times when there was inadequate assistance. She was not just friendly and supportive even in her lowest moments, but her faith was a comforting light situated deep within her as the darkness appeared omnipresent.

Finding God's Grace During Struggles

Over some time, I began to perceive my mother's love through a distinct perspective, one that was embedded within God's schematics and philosophies. She endeavored to sustain optimism when neglect was all but a certainty. Whereas when shame indicated that a life of mine was helpful, my mother hoped God would have something more pragmatic for me than this 'present generation' has to offer. In other words, "God is highlighting our strength, which is needed to manage bigger problems in the future," my mother replied. While gazing at her, I noticed a mix of exhaustion and affection in her eyes. It then struck me, Frantz- my mother always insisted that we are instruments of God even in dire situations instead of being the victims of our circumstances.

Discovering My Identity Beyond Rejection

Over the years, I appreciate that God used my mother's tenacity and strength to mold me. It began with her, with the yearning and gift of life, of faith and hope of a better tomorrow, and the willpower to endure the agony of being emotionally abused and exploited. Those early formative years of mine were not the best option, but they had their fair share of divine inspiration to direct the course of my life.

And in Haiti, when a child is born, they say: Mwen soti nan fènwa pou m' klere— I come out of darkness to shine. My life had begun in darkness. It was pure violence, and I am disgusted by all the rejection I faced. How is it easy to forget your mother's most vital teachings? Her indomitable faith instilled in me that it is not the end of the line. On the contrary, that is the prologue where God's light will most reside and shine.

My mother embarked on a small boat in April 1980 from Haiti to seek a better life for my siblings and me. She first had quite the adventure. She faced challenges along the way, which took away the delight of being at sea and her initial sense of hope, love, and excitement. The boat was broken and landed in Cuba. But she was treated with kindness and hospitality after being helped to build the ship and receive food. The journey then accelerated towards Miami, practiced and guided by the Cubans she met.

Eventually, American patrols came across them, and my mother and others were ushered to Miami. That was when everything started to change for her. Her story is challenging and love-filled: a woman who would do anything to ensure her children did not suffer like she did. My mother is an outstanding, brave woman who stood her ground and braved the world for her children to prosper.

When my mother became a lawful permanent resident of the United States, she embarked on the daunting journey of applying for green cards for us, her children. Her perseverance has brought its rewards, and in 1994, I was able to immigrate to the United States with her, thus reuniting the family and allowing us to start a new life together.

Like everyone who wanted to migrate, I, too, carried a bundle of dreams when coming to the United States. These were dreams to be respected, valued, and appreciated in this society and, with time, to be successful. Like every parent, my mom made a few impossible sacrifices for us. While beside my mom, I realized why those sacrifices and hard work were made. Her dreams became my dreams. I would see things from her. She built words into the world. Through her grit, I understood how the hardest of ways can lead to the most beautiful endings.

An Example of God's Plan:

Everything, I repeat, everything was embedded for a reason. From having to believe in a world deprived of ideologies, God ensured that whenever my mother's turn came, everything she went through and every sacrifice she made was meant to prepare me for a world filled with love rather than hate. Everything was destined.

By sharing her story, I cherish all the people who have been rejected but still try to love, have hope, and have faith that there is goodness beyond all suffering. Everything I consider a struggle in my life now was only life's challenges. I used to feel God's support was non-existent, but that was the case. Then, my mother's courage made me think we can never be 'alone.' There is always hope in God's love, even when there is nothing to hope for.

Life, which could have been considered unwanted, found scripts with Jesus coming to cover my nakedness. That reminds me that every horrible beginning can be transformed by God for His good, for us to win, for us to provide us with grace and the guts to risk everything in the hope of a new day.

CHAPTER 3:

An Unlikely Protector - The Strength of My Mother's Love

My mother was only fifteen years old when she decided to have me. Love and purity were within her, her being a hundred times pure. It was love, but love of a kind that was unconditional and even had a touch of time to it. She was so young, helpless, and unfit for motherhood, but there was this lioness protective instinct in her, and she was always there when I needed her. I can come up with a million words about her as a lady, but her will and relentless acts for my survival define her the best. A bright heart encased in an iron, throbbing heart of love, which I was destined to take off from.

Motherhood Started Early

When I think back on her journey, I draw strength from the power and courage she holds within. At fifteen, most children are idealists, but my mother was repeatedly forced to be pragmatic. She had to endure much pain back-to-back due to being a mother, but she did not lose hope and patiently took one step after the other to achieve her dream of being a mother.

In our society, she had to withstand society's scrutiny and was under the radar as a woman making her life decisions in front of our villages multiple times. She would constantly be ridiculed but remained unfazed and confident as the world continued to 'slander.' But my mother did not yield to their deceit and worked on herself to become strong and do her best to shield me from their brutality.

This dedication and devotion brought her downfall. She would go to extremes in every decision and in every work that she did. Her sacrifice was for me so I could have peace and be treasured despite all the trials and tribulations.

Enduring Tragedy

As far as I have noticed, my mother silenced every stern critic with ferocity. Losing so many people in her life only encouraged her to care for us even more. My mom ensured it was done if there was a need to work several long and tiring hours as a nurse's aide or do an additional shift or shifts. She made her family a priority in every place she visited. Even if this meant turning to such hurdles was required, she was ready for it.

That night, my mother was in tears. We had extraordinarily little, but she would even come out and arrange the few leftover groceries in the house. She earnestly asked me to eat a lot so I would be satiated and the cry within me subdued. I recall that night; it was rude of me because she scattered her food so I could have a nice meal. I did not realize that loving someone could be as much of a hassle when it came to empathy until I tried to find this love in her art of struggle. I was already old enough to understand this.

Moreover, I had an energetic mother doing all the things I may feel her affection for without a father figure. She also worked exceptionally hard because she wanted me to have everything regarding social respect and value, so she motivated herself to go real every day and work extra. After all, she went to great lengths to ensure I never felt like an outsider as I settled in Anse-Rouge. Consequently, I was the first who rode the bike, wore sneakers with some air soles, and put good-looking T-shirts on everywhere.

My mother worked hard and believed in herself. Her sacrifices paid off as I continued to reminisce about the dazzling experiences, such as biking around in my neighborhood and getting the attention I needed. Like any other person, she bought a man's bike rather than a woman's, and everyone around her was encouraged and motivated. Her sympathetic characteristics, riding a bike confidently, were shredding too many, especially women in our society. Her actions told them, "I will do whatever it takes to provide for my children, and I do not care about people's impressions." It was straightforward: "I will take care of my kids, and I do not care what people think." During her spare time, she even learned how to drive a tractor, saying that no limits prevented her from being masculine. There is no doubt my mother was a pioneer, and this was the turning point, which is why she taught me true love, struggle, and determination.

I was born in the General Hospital in Port Au Prince, the capital city of Haiti. My mother had decided to leave Anse Rouge, where she resided with her mother as a young girl who aimed at doing a lot. She was into trade as a merchant and used to hustle for capital. It occupied her in various parts of the blood, that is, Haiti. Also, I accompanied her everywhere she was working, placing me in many places. These trips were the first building blocks of my self-confidence and creativity because everywhere I went with my mother, we went into the busy areas and markets and the busy with so much trade and haggling around me.

During all this time, my mother concentrated on finding new opportunities in the US while I was still schooling at

Port au Prince. During the school holidays, I would go to Anse-Rouge, where I would trace my roots and see family. These admirable qualities made me have more respect for the rest of the family who tried to take care of me with such distances. My survival through all these transitions lies in how my mother suffered and coped wherever we stayed during those times.

Wisdom in the Eyes of a Young Mother

While my mother was young, to say the least, she had only a few wisdoms, and I remember how to have faith, respect, kindness, and resilience within the deepest part of my character. When things were calm in the evenings, there were occasions when she sat beside me to share stories about the importance of education, the value of hard work, respect for others, and doing the right things regardless of any situation. While she might have appeared quite soft speaking simultaneously, her voice and actions had a specific tone. She expressed her thoughts well: what we are now, our geographical situation, or how our life status does not define us.

Most people would consider that a struggle. My mother believed a battle was an intention, and there were many ways to achieve it. She would say, "Frantz, there is strength in our struggle." "We will get to the point in life where all events will happen for a reason, and then you will understand the meaning behind one struggle because that was meant to prepare you for something bigger," as per her "bigger goals." However, in all the sequences of events in life, she turned around and made them even better by whispering words within my ears. The hurdles in life are nothing but there to show how great and more extensive the goal is at the end of it all. All thanks to words from my mother and the treatments she gave me made me inch closer to understanding that we were not left scattered; what was all knitted was much, much more significant than us.

When I look for Love in my mother, I see one struggle, a weapon unmatched in my life, in her. Her life was full of trauma and turmoil for me to take one extra step and make it big in my life. There are several instances in life where one may even consider oneself far from success, especially after knowing everything she had to endure. However, quitting was never one of her options. Instead, she was always full of expectations from the outcome, no matter how dire the circumstance was.

I was at the threshold where age was of no restraint to ask my mom the sole reason for her never losing hope in me; it was only a matter of time. She looked at me while crying, turned to me, and said, "Frantz, I live because of you. God put you in my care, and I thank God for that." It is this consolatory statement that has been pertinent in shaping my life. That also made the struggling woman in me understand that she lost the imprint of love not because it was her duty but because she was in love that surpassed the need of self, which is why it is evident that I was captivated by her adoring kindness.

I was assured that the world would be good to me as I had a supportive family because my mother put all her dreams from her childhood aside to bring me up well and provide for my future. She encouraged me to believe in God, work hard, and never forget the lessons she taught me about life.

The Strength of A Mother's Love

In the following years, I often recall my mother and her love for me, filling in the gaps in everything I have become. To me, she was not a fairy in my childhood stories; instead, she was a warrior who protected me against innumerable circumstances. Her all-inclusive, self-sacrificing love was one thing that redefined me and turned me into an ordinary man who was confident about himself.

Through her, I began to see that strength does not depend on age or the situation. No, it is a quality deeply embedded within a person and only rages outward when provoked. For me, my mother's love was my strength and inspiration, and even in fading circumstances, her immortal premise of strong ambition was living in me. While it all might have set off in struggles and as a challenge, it was intermingled with a love that would encourage me to venture into the great unknown.

Using bubbles as a theme in art may seem simple, but the complexity of this theme is intriguing and attractive, and it remains one of the favorite themes artists like to delve into. For me, my mother's love was my strength and inspiration; her legacy ambition of strength lives through me.

While it all might have started with struggles and as a challenge, it was combined with a love that would take me ahead. My mother worked so hard, showed me so much, and guided me so well that I realized that God's love can turn the most terrible situations into a shimmering and glorious tale regardless of the theater of conflict or challenges of life that are posed.

CHAPTER 4:

Growing in Absence - A Childhood Without a Father

The emotions of a man not being present in a child's life are so strong and gravitating that they seem incomplete and helpless. While my mother worked hard to make up for my father's absence, we both knew living without a father's role would be hard. Her love sufficed for many of my requirements but did not solve my concern regarding several emotional facets. As I matured, I was continuously left wanting more and trying to find that love and attention in the wrong places without even knowing I was doing that. This absence only caused me to feel alone, unloved, and unworthy of anything outside an unwelcoming close. I began seeking validation from unreal and irrelevant, hoping to get the guidance I was missing. Looking back, I believe the presence of a father would have made my growth a little easier to bear.

While growing up, a father figure has proven to give emotional steadiness while setting an example, which will be crucial in the child's journey in life. A father is an essential pillar of confidence and security for a child. His presence is vital as he helps to explain the child's worth and also helps to explain their place in society. A child without a father's presence will experience many challenges with self-worth and making good choices. Kids could learn how to view their self-esteem from the father's perspective, which always teaches them to view themselves as valuable. There is no doubt that the position and love of a father figure in the family significantly contribute to a child's mental health and social relations.

Searching for Identity in a Fatherless World

Having been raised in a single-parent family felt like carrying an invisible weight. I have been unhappy watching my peers enjoying family time while I do not see my dad by my side. Instead, I feel like I am on the sidelines, and all I crave is the same bond. I have often questioned the reasons I was so unique from others. My expansion grew from a specific sensation to an indefinite intangible absence.

At most times, I believed something that was not factual about myself. Without being counseled on my rejections, I began to lose assurances that I was worthy of any form of love or acceptance. It is remarkable how even a child can, at a tender age, take even the tiniest episodes of rejection or absence and make them a scale of who they are. A belief that I considered to be somehow correct, that I was, as such, unworthy, came to be my part of life.

In my childhood, I began to look for women, trying to find an escape from the pain of insecurity and deprivation of emotions that the absence of a father had created in me. That led to sexual perversion. It was a misguided attempt to find connection, intimacy, and a sense of belonging. In this quest for validation, I constructed a perception of women based on lust rather than mutual understanding. I was not afraid to visit girls' homes that had no father. However, in families where the father figure was present, I could feel and sometimes see the tension of the man's presence, and their authority automatically commanded me to behave better.

Slowly but surely, these circumstances changed my perspective on how a father – or any masculine character- should be viewed in the household. I started to appreciate the love, wisdom, and strength these figures possessed and how they used it for their families. The realization that dawned on me was that an affectionate father was also a nurturer who could help develop an emotional equilibrium in the family. Most often, fathers are the ones who provide for, protect, and nurture the family, advise them, restrict them, and serve as leaders. Their power helps the children sense their significance and learn valuable life lessons, including accountability, respectfulness, and honesty.

In the transition from childhood to adulthood, I understood that life without a father deeply imprints on me. However, a light illuminated within me as I matured to understand the impact a father figure could have brought into my life. Most importantly, I began to recognize the necessity of taking responsibility and the consequences of fatherhood for myself and other people's lives. In that context, it also fueled my resolve to stop the chain of being a fatherless man and eventually be capable of becoming a loving, enriching, and nurturing father figure to my children.

Filling the Void with Wrong Influences

As time passed and my adolescent self asserted dominance, the feelings of wanting positive attention began to seek place. In searching for positive reinforcement and a sense of connection, I shifted towards peers and older teenagers. Lots were great mentors but, unfortunately, had an unfavorable perspective. I tried to get their validation even when I knew it was wrong, which I often did. One day, a bunch of older kids asked me to go out. They told me they had something to do that would be interesting, so I thought, why not?

That evening, I was told to join some activities, which, at the back of my mind, I understood were excessive. I also felt exposed and unprotected, which pushed me to some extreme measures to prove myself more burdensome. Exciting as it was, it never gave me a sense of belonging and instead supported the idea that I was alone and lost.

I started to recognize how these seemed to pull away the values I had presumed my whole life to have thanks to my mother when the edges turned too far. The behavior is subtle, but the construction of these spheres in society made me feel helpless in that the only solution was the erosion of my character. I know that feeling of wanting to be accepted while wishing to remain who you are.

Becoming A Parentified Child

Rapidly maturing, being the first of my mother, I was forced to take on adult duties for my siblings. My mother resided in the United States, and it came with a price. A price that forced me to take care of my siblings and sacrifice most of my teenage years. In many scenarios, the parent parenting parts were merely rendered the secondary outcome, with the responsibility of their well-being fully transferred to me. Life for me began at that moment when I felt that my shoulders and head were too small to carry that much weight, but understanding the void our mother had left me, idleness was never a choice.

It never came as a surprise, as while my family members tried as much as possible, thankfully, my grandmother, aunts, and extended family did their best to fill the void, but my day-to-day activities remained neglected.

My mother transferred funds and other resources from the USA so we could suffice, and I was responsible for these funds as most of our needs were met. Looking back, I know I was a boy; I was not prepared always to carry this burden well. In our town, where the need is rampant, my overwhelming feeling was to be more charitable, to the point of depleting our immediate essentials. My mother planned it for me as she was a doer herself and provided an example. Kindness, compassion, and the power to give were qualities we were meant to have even from the back of the room.

However, I knew that stretching our resources occasionally made things difficult for my siblings, so my good intent did not always result in them getting what they required because I aided others. Looking back, more importantly, I was exposed early to putting others first while appreciating that balance has to be maintained. These were the years in which I gradually understood the concepts of service, compassion, and resilience while figuring out how these concepts could be a part of our family in a secure environment. Such early life experiences and other memories from my growing years stayed with me. They instilled in me the necessary power and self-denial that accompanies the role of head of the family and the degree of responsibility that a parent or a guardian bears as a role model.

The Loneliness of Fatherless Nights

On multiple occasions, I needed to roll up into bed and sleep, but a voice kept me awake, haunted by moments, frozen by suppressing cold. The primary inhabitant of my mind was stagnation, filled with emotions, longing, and other feelings that could not be expressed with words, and my father's absence filled the void. This imaginary world constantly plagued my thoughts: what if he were there to mentor me? What if he were there to listen to me, or the least he could have done was let me know that he found me admirable?

Attachment styles are critical in parental figures. The way mothers love is entirely different from the way fathers love. In my case, I had the vitality of a mother but still sought a father's voice at times. I felt like I was lost in the middle of nowhere in an ocean, sailing last because of waves of doubts. Most importantly, this improbability would define my choices, making me seek validation in bitter places.

Finding Self-Worth in the Wrong Places

As I did not have a firm sense of self, I began to see everything through how others perceived me. The circumstances of their oppressive judgment misconstrued my values, stripped my purpose, and deranged my happiness. I vividly recall an instance where less fortunate children mocked me at school for being born fatherless one day while other kids laughed and teased me. Their remarks were hurtful, and I kept replaying them repeatedly in my head for days like a scratched record.

As a result, I developed a fixation on the idea that I would have to convince myself that the world saw me as insufficient and, hence, dedicate my life to that focus. I engaged in various activities that would allow me to achieve or be commended for completing such tasks. I made myself available and relevant so that people would respect me, but that was not cutting it. The gaping hole within myself continually taunted me despite my attempts to fill it in.

A Lesson in True Identity

One of those afternoons, I came across an older gentleman from my neighborhood who was keen to notice me. This man had faith in Jesus Christ and knew something of the battles that I was going through. He recognized a need for mentoring and offered me shelter where I could voice my concerns and confusions. He said, "Frantz, you do not belong to the people in your life. You belong to the people who shape your life. Who you are is not geographically bound." Those words rang a bell. That man believes a father's absence or others' opinions did not define me, but the One who made me did. Over time, I began to see that my worth does not have to be worked for; it is a gift from God. I needed to earn nothing because I was a child of God who was equipped, appreciated, and had a purpose regardless of my records or who accepted me.

Grateful For Caring Communities

Several community members came forward to assist with my siblings' needs and I. Professors at school, parents of girls I was dating, friends, and extended family members all played a part in our lives, offering guidance, encouragement, and even material help. Therefore, "It takes a community to raise a child," more so for those of us raised without a father or mother figure. Every one of them provided something unique — some offered practical assistance, others provided words of wisdom, and still others provided just their presence, which was a source of peace. Their willingness to step in helped me develop a sense of belonging and taught me that family can sometimes extend beyond blood.

One instance of community care that has vividly stuck with me until today is when I was approximately twelve or thirteen. I went to a small boutique shop to buy a cigarette one afternoon. I had already had a cigar to start to smoke for the first time. A stranger would think I was a grown man looking for a cigarette, as this woman handed the cigarette to me without a question. But as I walked away, excited to try this talk I was trying to do, I took the cigar in my hand, took out a small portion, and lit it.

At that moment, a voice began to yell, "Ti Frantz, kisa wap fè la? Ou pa dwe fimen!" which means, "Little Frantz, what are you doing there? You should not be smoking!" That voice was the woman who owned the shop and did not want me to smoke, and I knew it. Overall, it is safe to state that the seller did not want me to try smoking. Then, the woman ran towards me with a belt in hand to do her utmost to correct my weak reasoning. I was fast enough to run faster than she could get me, but her actions made me think. I was not simply a customer to her; I was a kid in the eyes of a responsible adult who felt obligated to raise me with proper values. In hindsight, this was a defining moment in my life.

Once again, she played a vital role since, without her attention and intervention, I could have gone down the road that could have resulted in smoking and other more severe habits. That woman who decided to intervene, only because of her conscience and care for me, contributed in a very modest but meaningful way to my sustenance of a healthier lifestyle.

It is very pleasing to know that there are such people in the world to whom God is the Father, and such people in the world are those who cared for me as for their children. Their persistence in making me repent, showing me the right path, and following me with a belt has been essential to my success. These private events made me understand the meaning of community: it is not just a place of residence but a circle of people who care enough to take responsibility for you even when you do not want to acknowledge how much you need this.

Finding Fulfillment in Playing Soccer

Soccer helped me escape the harsh realities of life and transformed me into my most significant source of fulfillment in life. As I began engaging on the pitch, I was acknowledged and accepted in a way I could not find anywhere else. I loved the game, and the fans' cheers made me proud and confident. The game impacted my self-esteem; people started betting on me to score goals. That trust in me always motivated me to score as much as possible. The game gave me purpose, and for the first time, I felt the importance of my life in the sight of others.

Having made a name for myself as a talented player, I had ambitions of turning professional, as football was my passion. Soccer has a special place in my heart. Whenever I have the chance to play, I do it, so that is much more enjoyable. Questionable soccer has a side where I make friends and have a purpose in life. Soccer instilled in me hard work, teamwork, and commitment, which have continued to define me even in ways I would not have expected back then.

Emerging from the Shadow

Those occurrences in my early life slowly made sense as I entered my teenage years. But I also noticed that I could become better. I understood that my tale did not need to conclude with the hurt of being left alone in all depths of despair or the blunders I underwent while searching for myself. It was also possible to draw strength from those challenges, seeing them as part of constructing a new self within myself that could love and serve a God who has a purpose for me.

It took a lot of work. It is hard to unlearn so much about oneself. It even sounds comforting to accept that such things are true. On the other hand, it is comforting to know that it is okay to feel that you do not need praise or approval from anyone to think that you are enough. I am enough, and I always will be.

Welcoming the Father's Love

Without an earthly father, I found a new sense of belonging in my relationship with God. He fulfilled the role of a Father who loved, guided, stood by me, and helped me to recognize who I am and what I can become in this world. I started to hear His approval rather than seeking others and hearing Him instead of waiting for others. This bond became my anchor. A new understanding of life and how I could build my future became apparent. Most importantly, my life was never about the people who were missing in it. It was always about the people who stood by my side.

In an era of enormous challenges and hardships, God continues to lead, protect, and ensure hope as he unimaginably guides me. I pay attention to how He transformed neglect into a tale about redemption by utilizing every hardship as a building block to mold me into who I finally became.

Moving Forward with Purpose

Today, I can look back on that chapter of my life with gratitude. Though painful, it taught me resilience, empathy, and a deep understanding of the power of God's love. I now know that I am more than my beginnings, loneliness, or the mistakes I made. I became resilient or forced myself to be one. Most importantly, each of my lows, loneliness, and hardships gave rise to a new, more assertive me. Knowing that God loves me, values me, and has chosen me over many has become the heart of my being.

In sharing this story, I wish to inspire others and convey the critical message that you are never alone, even when it may feel like it without those who were meant to be around. Remember, God is our Father, guide, and constant source of strength. We find our true identity in Him—where we are valued, cherished, and made whole.

CHAPTER 5:

Lost and Searching - Struggling to Find My Way

Regardless of age, one's life experiences directly determine one's character. People view the world through the lens of their past, and it is only such an experience that humanity can possess to emerge more resolute. But the lessons life taught me as I grew into adolescence and adulthood were harsh, for lack of better words. I was about 13 years old, and no father or male guardian told me the difference between good and evil. I was trying to seek validation and, in the process, making choices that would make me feel even more lost, and by doing so, I hoped to understand something clearly at last that would give me hope. I mean, I was always told the world waits for no one. So, naturally, all the images that a young me had of a victorious me kept gathering another layer of pain, giving me a sense of significant disorientation and helplessness.

Poor Decision Making

Do not all kids, at some point or another, desire freedom that will allow them to go out in the open and find themselves? They do, and I was trying to do the same here.

But a stronger sense of responsibility was missing, which was there to be developed and learned. As I went around, I could see many people who lived lavish lives and what seemed enticing at the time. So, young, I wanted all that and a lot more, which seemed unattainable; I tried to stand firm and do what I had to and, most importantly, fit in. With such desires in my head, breaking the instructions my mother left me with felt natural, and I began seeing myself excusing her and thinking this was how life was meant to operate.

Looking back, I realize how foolish I was and constantly reflect on my dark past self. This wave of social pressure naturally tested the best of me when I reached the years when I could explore my boundaries. So, naturally, for a young, aspiring, ambitious male, negative thoughts of making rash decisions that would potentially compromise my character were creeping in.

I thought there was no harm in being in a group and keeping my personal space. Little by little, I began to ignore my ethics in all cases whereby I sought to conform to my social environment; that is, every single situation was a step further into the life that I did not want to live.

Those were minor choices made at first, which turned out to be vast and costly. I became involved in deeds and habits that I knew were terrible but desired to conform.

However, the craving for acceptance and thrill made me do everything, although I lost my integrity. Each time I walked further from my integrity, I stepped into another realm that was even worse and more dangerous, where I felt lost and had no control.

Broken Relationships while Searching for Acceptance

With the passing years, I tried to chase relationships. It is as if with every person I would manage to talk to, the outlines of the swallow loneliness would fade or get buried. But with every search, I end up in shallow, sometimes unattainable relationships or could not survive my desire for acceptance. As every relationship ended, I would spiral into an even more isolated state, only this time, that was a worse ache than the last. It makes me think, am I so poorly made that there is something fundamentally wrong with me? But one particular relationship lost that one particular that broke me.

To me, God was restoring everything I had reset by including materialistic people. I made sure to include someone in my life whether I knew them or not, but while masking myself with God, I only relied on that person, believing that they would help me recover, but only to look forward to some much sought-after closure. It took some time, but with that hope, I imagined things to improve, and everything in me sought the change. However, that could not happen – or if it did, it was insufficient. Too much time I had spent in hope and being bound with the words of being healed. It was bound to go wrong; feeling unity in loneliness was God's intended purpose, but I did not see that coming. These reasons, including why resilience became such a pivotal lesson for me, as the moments I spent getting rejected fueled me to look wider into the world. Emptiness became a feeling that turned into a void, and I began seeking deeper than I and any human can offer.

Reaching 'Rock Bottom'

Every choice I made dragged me towards the relationships that filled the search for dependency and self-destructed me as a union; it was where cracks of hollowness uncovered the chains of reality. I was fighting hard to be acknowledged – finding my true self, only to feel pain and confusion. My circumstances became unstable, and there was only fear; the void was beyond the scope of my imagination. I had hit the lowest of lows, and the burden of my errors and blunders had become unbearable. That is when it struck me that I could not get help only from myself.

One night, sitting on the floor in my room facing the intolerable bed I had placed myself in, I started processing the events and circumstances of my life. It was quiet in the most disturbing way, so much so that I found it hard to ignore the various choices I had in excess made to quiet the pain. And in that quietness, it dawned upon me that I was not well-equipped to make things different, either in will or intelligence. It was a hard realization, but it also led to a much more thorough submission.

I recall thinking of only one of the first benchmarks that was a step toward real prayer. The words poured out of my heart without delicacy or finesse. But they were honest, and they were raw. I desperately told God I did not know, 'Please, just anything, offer me direction!' I admit that I did not know what I was asking for, yet inside, I needed something more significant than my physical body. I could see a dim ray of light at the end of my tunnel, and it was all beginning.

Learning to Lean on Something Greater

What followed from that point forth could have been quicker, simpler, and more enjoyable. It was challenging because I had to forget specific options and choices shaped over the years into my fabric. Instead, I admitted I did not have to contend with such circumstances alone.

The feel of God's presence became more precise, a constant reminder that I was not treading this path alone. I started seeking wisdom, learning about faith, and understanding that my worth came from something far greater than the opinions of others or the mistakes of my past.

People who would function as mentors and guides now came into my life, offering me wisdom and support that contributed to a change in my mindset. Gradually, I began to start the process of recovery, no longer finding my meaning and purpose in the situations I faced but rather in my relationship with God. Each step was small, but with every one of them, I could sense that a part of me was slowly being corrected, and a portion of my breaks was being healed.

I discovered and understood that I had been seen, respected, cared for, and loved even in my lost state. The grace I found was not because of my victory, but because he had been there with me in struggles through all the wrong turns, broken relationships, and despair moments I had. Now, I started to create a meaning for myself that was not defined by my failures but by the determination of love and purpose that was always there.

Finding a New Direction

Discovering my true self has undoubtedly not been straightforward, and praying for assurance only helped instill the ambition to seek God on my own. Temptation always invited me to relive the dark days of my past, but working persistently reminded me of the voice that spoke to me without my acknowledgment: "I am the one governing your actions."

In this life, I have learned to let go of the desire to control situations around us, which has proven counterproductive. True power lies in accepting that we alone do not have enough strength and submitting to a greater force in love without conditions. I do not pretend that my story, which is still evolving, is a picture-perfect one; it is an account of reality - of the most significant concern and love seen in God, who seeks our attention amid the chaos in this world.

As I consider this phase of my life, I hope my story can be a light for others who feel lost, have made mistakes, or are struggling to find their way. If you search for meaning or question your self-worth, let these words resonate with you. There is a world beyond your experiences that is filled with possibilities. You could have done nothing that God's redeeming love cannot fix. He is there, even in darkness, just waiting to shine.

CHAPTER 6:

A Divine Intervention: Finding Jesus in 1986

There are instances when life's set path changes—when you think of them and know now that destiny changed your life course. It was 1986 for me, a year that I can term a 'signal for a new life' that I had never dreamed of but had my understanding reshaped. That was the year I met Christ; my spirit and person became forever new at that moment.

I had so much arrogance; I was barren and lost in life's concepts. I lived in a utopia; everything to me was how it was. I molded my life through what I experienced, the theories taught in society, and the illusion of having power over my fate. If only I knew this, I could have prevented the inevitable aftershock from eventually happening.

The Preacher's Words

One day, I received an invitation to go to church. There was a lot of worship that day, and I vividly remember a comforting presence at the place. I want to say that I was skeptical about the whole thing but was ready to ignore everything. The pastor spoke and opened by telling God's word, and his tone made me pay some attention.

People heard about God more as a side note or an idea, but it did not sit right for me. Every time the pastor spoke, I can now recall it as an unsettling experience, as though I was being put to the stand and exposed. A revelation dawned on me strong like a tsunami: I was living in sins against the God who created me and loved me. I was moving away from reality because of my pride, arrogance, decisions, and dependence on myself. At this moment, I was entirely off the mark. I had committed a crime against the One who created me.

And here is how it went down: My eyes started pouring in tears where there had been so many, for I had come to terms with the distance and the drift. My excessive pride came crumbling down, for the preacher's word had sounded strong for me, and the truth was now all I could see: that I was a sinner needing forgiveness. Little did I know that day would be the most profound and life-changing day of my life.

The Altar Call

The preacher extended an invitation: "Who would like to give their life to Jesus today?" At that moment, something shifted within me. I knew that I could not keep living this way. I knew I had to let Jesus in; this was my moment. So, I rose and moved towards the altar, making it there without a second thought.

I then prayed, and while doing so, I could sense my sin digging deeper into my skin. However, I was grateful for the chance to face the bright side. I spoke and made my confession clear, how I acted contrary to what God wanted me to do throughout my life. I asked for God to forgive me and let me start anew. As for me, I felt like a sinner, but as He said, "Let him who has no sin throw the first stone," so I put my trust in Jesus Christ, for he died to save me.

All the sins that I had been committing had been forgiven. When I finished my prayer, tranquility spread across my heart, comforting me as if everything were off me. I had been consumed by guilt, shame, and anxiety due to my mistakes, but it was always a matter of time before God showed mercy on me. It was not because I deserved it but because of his grace and mercy. That day, all I had done was not just utter a few words; it was a vow, and that was to enter a relationship with Jesus Christ. I was filled with a greater sense of joy and appreciation when I left the altar. I am sure I was given love, forgiveness, and, most importantly, freedom.

A Grateful Heart

I certainly felt differently after leaving the church that day. I could hear the pride, the arrogance, the emptiness—it was all fading away. I had been one of those individuals who walked with pride, but now I was coming out in gratitude and happiness, for I had been given another chance. I no longer existed for myself or was a prisoner of my sins; I lived for God and, in a sense, became a child of His grace, which radically changed my life.

I had met God in a vulnerable state, and He made me whole again; he gave me restoration and purpose, too. I knew that life had something new for me the next day. And even as I recollect those memories, I am sure that was not just the start of something new but a new life wherein I was in Christ. For me, it was a day when I got a glimpse of God's love in its most accurate form, and ever since, I have seen a facet of love that has influenced me.

That day in 1986 was the best and most incredible day of my life—because that was the day I found Jesus.

My Mother's Son to My Mother's Shepherd

But to her surprise, she manages not to see the brighter planning aspects and purpose God so desperately wanted to present her with. He will seek out this skeptic child, the one born and parented out of wedlock, and proclaim that it will make her believe in the power of Jesus Christ. Today, I am not only her son but her brother in Christ and a pastor. Such things, the way God works, are pretty miraculous to behold.

Without a doubt, this illegitimate woman, who was once scorned by society, became the very reason my mother's heart yearned for Jesus. He has blessed me in so many ways. My existence, career, and duty are part of his divine purpose of setting, restoring, and transforming our family. Now, being her pastor, it is a great blessing for me to encourage her faith and assist her in fulfilling the promises of God. A myriad of times, we assist the Lord at Love Kingdom. What a disheartening thought – that the child who had caused her so much suffering is now able to help her spiritually bolster, support, and assist her.

I am honored to have such a lovely mother. My mother is also the mother of the church. Her love, self-sacrifice, and zeal to serve God and his people are shown everywhere. There is so much empathy in what she does, how she chooses to serve, and how she cares for everyone around her. Her work speaks for her devotion to the Lord.

Our contact has developed beyond mother and child as co-laborers in Christ on a journey to answer God's purpose. I serve God at Love Kingdom, and she has assumed the role of 'mother' in our Church. She provides love and care and meets the demands of His people with a heart filled with love. Her transformation from being a source of shame to one of grace and from being in despair to having a purpose can be described as unfathomable. She has been and continues to be an inspiration of faith and strength to the people in our community.

I will always be grateful to you, Mother. Thank you for everything that you have done for me and the Church. Your dedication and love have embodied God's will, and it is a privilege to consider you my mother and a fellow in the gospel.

CHAPTER 7:

The Meeting That Changed Everything - Encountering My Father

Certain historical scenes remain vivid in our minds and hearts and define us most unexpectedly. I experienced something of this nature when I was twenty-four. It was a day I had dreaded but also looked forward to. That was the day I finally met my father, whose absence from my life had haunted me for as long as I could remember.

I created many versions of who he was in my mind- who I was made to be and why he was not around me. Anger, curiosity, and sadness at my father's absence led me to formulate all these versions, the ultimate question: Why is he not here? This sweet and sour mix of emotions defined me during my formative years. The fullness of meeting him, however, aggravated my anxiety and excitement simultaneously. Would I finally get my answers after waiting so long? Or even closure?

The Reunion, which was Both Shameful and Joyful

For many reasons, it is safe to state that I was looking forward to reconnection. Nonetheless, the reality of reuniting with my father dawned on me after so many years. Everything became far too awkward and tense to understand, but enough was said to make some meaning. That has been one of the best transitions of my life.

As I walked into the room where we were to meet, my heart pounded with anticipation. My father was a man I had never known yet who had profoundly influenced my life. Looking at him, I expected to find a face I had grown to imagine in my head. I aimed to witness the real-life version of the man I had created, but I was puzzled. We exchanged formalities, not knowing what to say after all these years. There was this burning wish in my heart that made sense of my dad, and I made a significant effort in that direction because he was the one, after all, who had been absent in my life but had played a key role in many aspects of my life. It is not even after saying much, but at least two words, 'I'm sorry,' that would have provided a sense of justice to my childhood that was well shattered.

His words could have made my childhood memory crumble even more, and I was worried about that. He accused my mother of everything. She misunderstood; she chose to make decisions, and because of that, she cut him out of my life. I felt like a volcano of resentment would erupt, revealing the injustice that had been felt all this time. That was the most challenging thing to accept; my mother was the one who tried her best. She had taken on the role of both mother and father, meaning she had to raise me alone. I remember how extreme measures had to be taken to love and support me. It was hard to fathom how people would lay blame on her while she was the one who had been in pain the most in my entire life. I am surprised that I did not end up getting violent; complete disregard for violence would have been suitable under the circumstances.

Wrestling with Anger and Pain

I was filled with many emotions, a chaotic mess inside my head. There was a part of me that wanted to explode and lash out at everyone around me, to defend my mother and let my years of suppressed rage go free. But a similar part of me was mourning and disappointed and even felt shame and embarrassment, which made my body shudder with confusion. To my relief, I was about to meet the man who was going to be a husband to my mother; he would have been the perfect remedy for my painful experiences. However, he was now only going to add to my pain.

I closed my eyes to calm myself down, struggling with violent thoughts. After all, my father did not do anything that was out of my narrative; however, he did quite the opposite and was willing to help me rewrite the narrative. I knew that revealing my rage could help me in the short term. However, anger management would not be able to address the agony I had been going through for so long and the questions that cropped up in my mind.

A Path Toward Forgiveness

After that first meeting, I struggled a lot due to the mix of emotions: anger, disappointment, sadness, and, surprisingly, also some form of relief. Meeting my father was a significant event in my life, as this person had taken his time to unlock the majestic answers to my life. However, this was still painful and challenging. Rather than being a man of elusive explanations or my imagination, he was just a normal human being, having dreams but with misfortunes and regrets.

As the days passed, I focused more on forgiving someone for their wrongs. I focused on forgiveness to lose the past I was struggling to forget, so all the anger and resentment I held on to for so long vanished. I did not have any animosity towards my father anymore; it was all about forgiving for the sake of allowing my heart to heal.

I began praying to refine my approach towards my father and help myself for a better tomorrow. Resentment is not a positive sentiment, and I agree that it would block my relationships, peace, and purpose. I would not like to get old with such bitterness, but on the other hand, I wanted to be able to forgive past mistakes so that I could concentrate on more important life issues.

Healing Through Understanding

Over time, I slowly started to understand my father. I had neither justified his behavior nor felt the nagging anger I had previously towards his actions - I felt trust instead that there was a good reason for his actions. I understood that sometimes people erred not out of evil intent but just out of weakness, fear, or lack of understanding. I also began to see that my quest did not involve looking for a model father but looking for the right attitude and determination to mold the past the way I wanted.

My mother's unconditional support and affection have always been the anchor in my life, the absolute strength. Women's love and devotion have turned me into the emerging me, molding me into a man of all attributes. And yes, the lack of my father in my family has been unbearable; however, it is also part of my life, a part of my life that has made me appreciate every single person who has been there. This journey of forgiving was challenging and was not done in a day.

That was not easy, nor was it overnight. It took rekindling my faith, a collection of prayers, and, more importantly, the will to confront the skeletons in my closet that I had locked away for so long. However, every effort brought me closer to betterment, to a much-needed closure that I really cherish, as it has, in all honesty, helped me come to peace with my past.

A Brief Encounter, A Lifetime of Questions

What I did not realize then, sadly, is that flash of a moment we shared, our last encounter on my paternal side, was also, in fact, the final encounter of the father I had been dreaming about all this precious time. Witnessing the first meeting in and of itself was a contested one, an opportunity to gather mixed feelings about me, their complex entity claiming to be my father yet being so bizarrely distant. There were an infinite number of questions I wanted to ask him. I had been waiting ages for the right opportunity to ask him numerous questions. However, our interaction was sadly too short-lived, so I left unease that we still had so much more to say but never got the chance to.

I never imagined that when we first crossed paths, or rather, when I last saw him, would also be the only time I would ever set my eyes on my father again. It was far too difficult of a challenge to sit and build all the lost time, and from that point onwards, only regret followed; truth be told, we never had the chance to fully develop the bond I dreamed of forming. It was as if a chapter in my book had just been forcibly closed, leaving unfinished business and a feeling of unfound loss I never expected.

Six months later, my father was dead. But how difficult it was! This man whom I never knew, how could he be capable of such influence? I grappled with the intricacies of grief, not only of losing my dad but also some of the questions of which I would have to remain in ignorance. Why did he not come into my life all those years? Had the forces been different, what would he or I have been like in our times?

While I would not have had the chance to grow up with him, I learned a valuable lesson: In such instances, one's life can be changed by the shortest meetings. While the emotional pain of his absence remains, it also took me to places that I had no idea I was already in. His death compelled me to explore truths about life, loss, and being a father even as I started living in a world minus him. While this was a painful chapter, it encouraged me to appreciate the time and the people around me.

Embracing a Deeper Purpose

There was this incredible art inside me, waiting to flourish. It was only when my father was facing me that I realized that purpose was inside me, and my purpose was something beyond measuring, as I understood the purpose was more comprehensive than what my father had been doing. A sense of focus had begun to engulf me, as evidently, I knew what this life had to offer, and that was nothing but scrolling through my past filled with persistence and more persistence.

This novel act unfurls the emotion of vent and balance. As I stated above, what I went through with my father was not frustration or desperation due to the lack of understanding that had been set up within me. That helps me frame the sense that anger is a one-time act and might set me on a journey to be calm. Perspective is critical; I had honed perspective. If I could not change the mind of one, I could at least be opting to change the perceptions of the words. In situations like this, offering an apology on their behalf was easier said than done, so again, throughout history, it had always been easier to say sorry and move on.

After encountering my father face to face, I embraced calmly and collected. A new flame of appreciation blossomed in me since this was an entirely new perspective for me, the perspective of being quiet and understanding rather than letting my mother influence and shape such ideas that would always have been spoken and acted with patience and understanding. Regardless of the pain and offering silence for the sake of pain caused by nothing, stories were stored, fearing that I would be a sound loin carrying the burden. Surviving through situations like meeting my father or my reality of this core desire helped me become the person for whom I had always longed.

It brought me nearer to the reality of who I am, to the acceptance of my story, and, most importantly, to the understanding that healing is always an option, and so is hope, even in the most challenging pages of one's life. My story was about resilience, finding strength in unexpected places, and learning to let go of the past to embrace the future.

Meeting my father may not have been what I had hoped for, but it was exactly what I needed. It brought me closer to understanding who I am, finding peace in my story, and recognizing that there is room for healing and hope even in the most painful chapters of our lives.

CHAPTER 8:

Forged in Faith: The Discipline of God's Word

My first interaction with Jesus was the most vital moment of my life. It made me feel joy, such that I had never felt before. But I had areas in my life, thoughts, and even habits that I could not instantly change. It was as though I was rekindled into this world, only to be clueless about certain aspects. My only passion was one concerning the changes, but I could not let go of the existing. I could not stop myself from determining my objectives based on my wants, and although I had a 'conscience' able to discern right from wrong, I could still not bring forth that change that I longed for. I started feeling the stress of expectations, one of which pertained to coming to terms with the changes concerning my ambitions. I felt as if I was sandwiched between two lives. One was my old self, and one was unknown, as I had no way to pursue my new ambitions.

    I have realized that my conflict resulted from ignorance. I had received salvation, but I had never been taught how to walk in the fullness of everything that Jesus gave. I was in that deficiency; I did not know how to live in the teachings of Jesus, the principles of the Kingdom, or the power of the Holy Spirit. I was, however, pouring my energy into efforts at changing myself while floundering without an inner sense of motivation. I had not yet come across the core principles that made it possible to have a transformation, which are concealed in the pages of the Bible and made accessible through His Spirit. I did not realize that the absolute basic tenets were buried somewhere between the lines of God's word and could only be found by His Spirit.

The Turning Point: Embracing the Discipline of God's Word

An unusual event unfolded in 1997. I came to a time where I became so fed up with wanting to try and fail again, to put in tremendous effort and expect changes that would be permanent. There was this strong urge not to open my Bible here or there merely but to open it more or less every day and search for the truth. I promised myself to read the Bible, saying I would read Genesis to Revelation so that the word of God could dwell richly in my mind and heart. It ceased to be a matter of obligation or colonialism, but such a desire to know God, to hear His words, and to understand the life He designed for me was more excellent.

Prayer and fasting also took center stage in my faith pilgrimage. These activities were my means of shutting the world out and focusing on the creator. I sought the help of the Holy Spirit so that He could unfold what I had read and help me live according to what it said. I learned that the Bible was not only a history book or a set of laws but a bouquet of love and life instructions, a power source.

Every time I read the Bible, I see a new aspect of God's character and love for me. I am gradually being transformed into someone who can conform to his ways.

God's Word Has the Strength to Make One Change

Since 1997, I made a point to read the Bible, starting from Genesis to the Book of Revelation, and I already read it over a hundred times. This practice of the kingdom has been a remarkable influence in my life as it has opened my eyes to the wide range of available resources through Jesus Christ. I have now started to fully appreciate and experience the concept of salvation in its fullness, not as something to be wished for but a reality to relish as one that brings glory to God by soaking my heart and mind with scriptures.

So far, I have not only had the experience of reading a sacred scripture but am particularly captivated by what Jesus and his apostles say in the New Testament. These have been compartments of wisdom, directing and guiding me through knowing and following Jesus daily. With the grace of the Holy Spirit and prayer coupled with fasting, I have liberated myself from the shackles of my past. Otherwise, that is, without the practice of studying God's Word, I would still be enslaved to my passions, the desires of my flesh, and the deceptive influences of the world, including its fleeting trends and demonic traps.

I strive to make reading the Bible an enriching experience on a personal level, one in which God becomes more recognizable. The practice is alright, and it's more than alright because it enables me to have positive dominion over my life, instills me with faith and hope, and rebuffs temptations I once succumbed to without a fight. Reading the Bible is not an activity for me but a calling. The calling is to foster within me, every single day, the hope enabling me to be in the world and God's Kingdom.

This aspect has crystallized in my mind that transformation is embedded in the daily reorientation of an individual's life, both internally and externally. The word of God is not simply literature to be marveled at; it is a practical guide to everyday life, real and functioning. It is constantly working in me, aiming to touch and distance all to allow me to highlight His glory as He planned.

The Power of God's Word and the Holy Spirit

As I continued doing this, I discovered that the instructions given by Jesus were not just meant to be observed as rules but more like daily spiritual food to reflect the character of God as a citizen of his kingdom. I began to appreciate the concept of kingdom living, which revolves around love, forgiveness, humility, and faith. The narratives of the people of God and the hand of Jesus became an aviator on how my life and lifestyle were shaped, pushing me to change my strategy. I felt God bless me with lofty expectations with every passage, and instead of scolding me, He invited me to rise to the standard he hoped for.

He began to be part of my complexion, support, and power. It struck me that Christ is not a caregiver far away; he is my best friend. He comforted me in periods of spiritual and physical weakness. He gave me answers when I needed guidance. I then shifted my focus during temptations and relied on him instead of just wanting to use my willpower.

Descending to my knees proved fruitful as I understood what it meant to walk by the Spirit. I realized how much I realized how much I depended on Him for every single thought, word, and action. As I surrendered, He took the raw material of my life and, through His Spirit, added new strength and peace so that it would conform to the image of God I was deeply predestined to.

A Life Transformed By Discipline and Devotion

I experienced God through the Bible every second of my life. It was as if, with every reading, I was equipped with new strength and a new understanding of peace. I monitored conforming to the old patterns of my mind and replaced them with God's word. My gnostic arrogance and self-righteousness melded into gentle humility, genuine love, and the required patience. My desires were liberated. Where once I sought carnal lust, I was transformed into hoping for the greater good and seeking God constantly. It is a development that is hard to describe, but every day, I felt less and less of who I was, an inch closer to who God wanted me to be.

This devotion to seeking God through his Holy Word and Prayer became the foundation of everything I did. It kept me stable wherever I went and in whatever awful situations I might be stuck in. The Word of God rendered me secure whenever temptations would challenge me.

The values I have today, my choices and my peace are all rooted in this. The core principles that stand on the bedrock of scripture and are carried forward by the Holy

Spirit's presence used to be nothing but emptiness, lack of purpose, and brokenness.

The Profound Impact of God's Word: Finding Healing and Wholeness

Thus, the living word of God for me was not just a change of action but a change of the heart. It caused me to be defined and described by God's love, grace, and provision. I found out that I was secure in His love, for I was wanted and valued, but this did not have anything to do with what I had done, but instead, what Jesus did for me, and this began to shift my whole view on life. I no longer had to be ashamed or insecure; I could live confidently and joyfully. I became more Christ-like or saw things through God's eyes, gave grace to others, and served.

In every situation and every decision I faced, the Bible was able to be my guide. It provided me with wisdom when I needed it concerning relationships, confidence when I was facing challenges, or courage when I was in despair. It instructed me on how to love, how to forgive, and how to place my trust entirely in God as well as trust people. With time, I have understood that wholeness and healing are not achieved through a struggle or fight for it but rather through aligning oneself with the truth of the Father.

Throughout my life, the growth I have gone through started with my beliefs, the ideals that I stand by, and the inalienable rights that one seeks throughout one's life.

A Call to Embrace God's Word and Find Transformation

My experience only proves the benefits of God's words and the Holy Spirit. I would be thrilled to persuade the readers of this chapter to do this, take it as a call, and embrace the Scriptures as an instrument of knowing God in his love and feeling the truth that will change them. For anyone who thinks he is stuck in a vicious cycle, I want to tell you that there is hope and the possibility of freedom. That is the purpose of God's Word in your life; through his Spirit, it can work in you, and so will your life.

I, for one, have been applying the discipline of reading the Scriptures, praying, and relying on the Holy Spirit, where both understanding and rationale have brought love, peace, and gentleness to me and to serve others. It has transformed me from despair to triumph, from pain to soothing calmness, from working too much to no effort. The same offer I extend to those willing to change their life around, start seeking God with all they have by turning their hearts towards him, building their life upon his words, and surrendering to the Holy Spirit. Through the sacrifice of our self-will and the work of our sacred souls, we can discover the life we were meant to lead and the faith we are bound to give—a life full of inspiration, happiness, and timelessness.

Discipline and devotion will lead us to a life of meaning, happiness, and eternal value, which the Lord God created for us.

CHAPTER 9:

A Vision for Love: Embracing God's Purpose

I must say that discovering what I was meant to do in life has been a lifelong journey of discovering God's plans for me. My loving relationship with God improved as I continued delving deeper into the scripture and relying on the Holy Spirit. I realized that my existence on this earth was not only for self-transformation. I started feeling God telling me to go out and speak his truth and turn people towards hope and love. That was a significant transition for me – instead of looking inward for change, I was looking outward for change that I could bring about in others.

The Call to Ministry: Advocating for God's Purpose

For years, I wrestled with the idea of stepping into ministry. I had many doubts about my worthiness, ability, and understanding. As I emphasized, it is about worth and whether one is equipped for the task alongside the understanding part. A multitude of fears encompassing my spirit were annihilated in an instance when I turned to prayer.

There were desires that I had to put aside and instead adopt the vision to focus on what God wanted. He had a plan for me in which I was to work towards building His Kingdom through love, leading people to Jesus, and giving them purpose in Him. It was quite a humbling experience as it meant losing everything and trusting in the process. That was going to be tough. However, there was a kind of peace ensuring me that I was pursuing the purpose of GOD in my life.

Once, a pastor's son foretold that I would become a pastor, and he would serve as a church secretary. I remember mocking the suggestion as something entirely impossible for me. To join the roars of laughter, I added, 'If I ever become a pastor, I will steal all the money the church has, and we both had a good laugh.'

What appeared to everyone as a jest, the future tense, transforms the tone and meaning, which now is like a pronounced word that got the better of me- one which, over the years, found its expression. When I look back, I see how the seed words of God reached out to me even though I did not know God's face and voice. In that instance, he was preparing the ground for the path He had prepared for me. He told me I have far more purpose for your life than you could ever imagine. That is a lesson on how life always does not proceed as intended, for God is great at doing the unexpected. All too easily, one forgets how many opportunities are missed due to blind faith and a lack of awareness.

1997, I prayed and fasted, seeking God's guidance about attending Bible college. I felt the Holy Spirit prompting me to enroll at Hope Sound Bible College to pursue a degree in pastoral ministry. On the eve of registration, I had just one cent on me, which was far from meeting the school's registration fees; therefore, I slept feeling confused. However, I managed to have a dream that night. During that dream, I was reminded of how God called Abraham, and now here was God commanding me, saying, 'Go to the school.' So, the next day, I acted according to that command but was still clueless about how I could afford college. In a bizarre turn of fate, I went in faith, and there, someone handed me his checkbook and told me to write what I needed to cover my registration fees.

Owing to how hard I worked for my degree, I graduated in 2001. I was one blessing after another blessing. Before my graduation, I visited Israel, and this voyage was bound to be full of epiphanies, granting me the desire to intertwine the historical God with the many stories related to him across various ancient places. After graduation, I married my sweetheart, Djenny, in 2001 at a serene and modest wedding in the presence of God, family members, friends, and fellow believers in Christ.

A Moment of Integrity and Forgiveness

However, shortly after my wedding, I encountered a trial. My pastor requested to have a meeting with the church board. During the meeting with the pastor and some church board members, I poured out my heart to them, moved by the prophet Samuel's parting address to the people of Israel before he retired from active leadership over the nation. I was very much touched by Samuel's words and his way of discussing things because I wanted to go with the same level of honesty that he possessed.

I said, "I have been a member of this church for some years now, and I would like to remind you that this is the only church I have known since I arrived in America. Should I have embezzled funds, participated in illicit activities, or committed any offense against the Lord's word, this might be the right opportunity for you to clarify all that. I am prepared to accept responsibility, apologize, and correct my wrong ways."

Their response was short and to the point: "You did no wrong. It is just that we do not require your services in that church anymore."

Hearing those words, I felt the weight of rejection, but I refused to let bitterness or anger take root in my heart. With courage and peace, I responded, "Let God be the judge between us. Let His will be done. I forgive you, and I love you."

The room fell into a profound silence. No one spoke, and the atmosphere was heavy with unspoken emotions. I stood, shook their hands, and embraced them before walking out. It was a moment of release, not just for me but, I believe, for them as well.

Although it was difficult for me to depart from the ministry and the church of God I had loved and served for so long, there was an inward calm. God had gone with me to take me through a new season, and that particular moment made me appreciate the significance of forgiveness and enjoy its liberation. There was no need to convince someone or justify one's worth; it was already clear that God was in control, and all that was needed was to move on as a winner.

Lessons in Leadership: Becoming a Servant of God's People

Reflecting on the painful episode with the pastor and church board, I realize God used that moment to mold my character and prepare me for subsequent events. It was a personal challenge and a rehearsal for what was in store for me. It was God's divine purpose, which has become more apparent with each passing day and each new event in my life.

Through their actions, I learned **not to treat people as a leader.** Their decision, made out of jealousy and insecurity because of how God was using me at the church, was callous and demonstrated how influential a leader can be, sometimes to the detriment of nurturing a relationship. It also made me understand the immense sense of responsibility a pastor has to ensure that he guides God's people with love, dignity, and compassion.

This experience taught me **leadership is not about power or control but love and service.** A true leader carries the people's burdens, listens to their concerns, and seeks God's wisdom in every decision. I vowed that if God called me to lead His people, I would not follow the same path of coldness and rejection.

Instead, I vowed to **lead with love, service, and humility.** God was working in me, helping me understand that every person is worthy of respect and must be treated with the love of Christ. I understood that leadership is a high and holy trust that must be exercised in loving the Lord and His people, not self-seeking goals or hierarchal dominance.

This painful chapter became my starting point for a pastoral ministry philosophy—a Christian leader should be a humble, loving, and hardworking servant of the people of God without seeking fame or popularity. I am thankful because that lesson gave me the wake-up boost to lead others in living Christ's heart daily.

Choosing Unity Over Division

To prevent any feud or quarrel in the church, I had to make the painful choice to leave the pastor and church board to substantiate the grounds upon which I was excommunicated. I could have spoken out, but my heart was more preoccupied with the oneness of the whole church. I did not want anyone blessed by what the Lord was doing in me to consider leaving the church as an option in protest. There is much more work to be done in God's Kingdom than in any individual case, and I believe He would come through with the right decision at the right time.

However, some church members felt hurt and confused by my silence. They thought I had betrayed them by not sharing what had happened or asking them to join me elsewhere. I understood their perspective—their frustration came from a place of love and loyalty to what God had been doing in their lives.

In time, I could explain why I had chosen to remain quiet to those who approached me. I shared my conviction that dividing the church would dishonor God and His work. I reminded them that the church belonged to God, not me, and that my focus was obedience to Him, even if it meant enduring personal pain.

As they listened, their hearts softened and began to connect the dots. Numerous praised God for the lesson of humility and trust that I could exhibit even in such a moment.

This experience deepened my conviction that leaders must prioritize the unity of the Body of Christ, even when personal sacrifices are required. I walked away from that chapter with a renewed faith in God's ability to bring good out of any situation and an unwavering commitment to place His will above my own.

The Start of a New Church

On 17th November 2001, confidence settled in as I joined two friends praying and fasting on Saturday 16th of November, requesting God for direction. But as the night fell and I prepared to retire, the nervousness settled in again because I was unsure where I would attend church the following day. That same night, I had another unsettling dream. 'I have consistently advised you to set up a church for my people, and you have continuously refused,' said an elderly figure. I asked, 'What do you expect of me?' He responded, 'I expect you to establish a church in your house. If you continue to disobey me, I will go out and evangelize the people.' That is, however, what I expected of you.'

When I woke up in the morning, I got ready as if I were going to attend a church. I had set chairs around a podium placed in my living room. No people were in attendance, but I trusted in God's presence. I began preaching on Galatians 6, specifically "How to Restore a Fallen Believer." As I preached, the Holy Spirit reminded me of Ezekiel 37:1-10, where God asked Ezekiel to prophesy to dry bones for the bones to breathe life. I prayed, saying, "Lord, I do not have dry bones; I have empty chairs." God spoke to my heart, "Touch the empty chairs and pray over them. I will fill these seats with people who must know the truth." I obeyed, and now, a new ministry was born out of faith.

Later that day, I shared the experience with my two friends, who prayed and fasted with me on Saturday 16th, and one of them joined me in starting the new church. Thus, the Holy Church of Grace was born on November 18, 2001. When my newlywed wife returned from a trip to Haiti, I told her about the church. She graciously joined me in this mission, and together, we committed ourselves to promoting God's Kingdom, grounded in love for God and love for people. Later, we renamed the church Love Kingdom to reflect this mission.

Looking back, God used my excommunication to lead me to His purpose. He guided me from a place of loss to where He wanted me to serve.

Leading with Love: Serving Others as Christ Served

I was sure I was doing the work of my calling. Only this time was it better because love participated in everything. Everything that Christ had done, His life, for example, his ministry, was characterized by compassion and humility, and there was great devotion in serving those in need. God kept reminding me to do the same, to promote love. That necessitated regarding people as he regarded them, exercising grace instead of judgment, and working without expectation of reward. What I knew afterward was that authentic leadership is service in humility.

In my ministry, I encountered people facing hardship, loss, and pain. God taught me that my role was not to "fix" them but to walk alongside them, pointing them to His healing power. Through this journey, I experienced a love greater than anything I had ever known—one that could break chains, heal wounds, and restore lives. It was a privilege to witness God's transformative work in others.

Helping Others Find Their Purpose

However, as I embraced God's purpose for me, I realized that my weaknesses were also my greatest strengths. I realized that I not only had power but great purpose in everything. I started seeing the world differently. God showed me other people's struggles within myself, and so I sought their answers and understanding from God.

One of the greatest mysteries is understanding how much pain people go through because life is a two-way street, balanced by anger and love. Given my life experiences, I can undoubtedly say God's love is genuinely restoring and redeeming.

I devoted myself to helping others experience the freedom and wholeness I had found. Through counseling, teaching, and pastoral care, I sought to be a source of encouragement—someone who would listen, pray, and remind people of God's promises. The joy of seeing lives transformed renewed my commitment to God's calling.

Fulfilling God's Purpose: Lifetime Devotion To His Work

Another lesson learned on my journey might be fervently held onto by many: there is purpose in every difficulty, and considering God's aim requires faith and perseverance. Without the abovementioned principles, it is safe to assume that my plans and visions would have taken precedence over where I should go. However, those slight changes became greater, bringing me closer to my true calling. It is about sacrificing yourself for others while helping others, even when it gets daunting.

When you think that I am done, let me burst your bubble. Understanding God's Setting is a never-ending process that necessitates daily attentiveness to him, traversing and believing in something far more significant than oneself. From then on, I understood that he had been marking my path, helping me strengthen my faith, and opening doors I thought never could be opened. My joy stems not from searching for my ways but rather from pursuing the will of the Father in heaven.

A Call to Acknowledge The Reason for Your Existence

So, looking back on this journey, I would like to invite you, my dear reader. God has a plan and a purpose for every individual, and it is always peculiar to each individual; that is, the calling is in their life. For some, it could be in the area of ministry; others are called to do business, raise families, or serve in the community. No matter the path, the foundation is the same: love. God commands us to love others as He has loved us, to serve with compassion, and to be willing to serve without seeking recognition.

If you have yet to find your life's purpose, seek God, be true, and do so sincerely. Follow the directions of His Word and the Spirit, and be sure He will let you know when the time is right. To have purpose may mean suffering adverse circumstances, but on the brighter side, this purpose will provide satisfaction and happiness to an extent only God can give. His love leads us to be empowered, for that is the ultimate purpose of our lives, to not live for ourselves but for Him and, in turn, for the benefit of humanity.

I pray that you may enjoy the same fullness in God's purpose for your life. May His love be the vision that guides you, the strength that sustains you, and the joy that fills your heart as you walk in His ways. Embrace the journey, and let God use you to bring hope, healing, and love to a needy world.

CHAPTER 10:

A Husband and Father–Learning to Love and Lead

How Did I Meet My Wife?

To explain how I met my wife, Djenny, I should start by apologizing for my past – something I am not proud of. As I now look back, it is evident that I was very much lost in the relationships that I had throughout my teenage years, lacking direction before finally God drew me to Christ. Things changed for me in 1997 when I entirely devoted my life to God after meeting Christ for the first time in 1986. I made a radical choice: I decided to avoid romantic relationships altogether instead of pursuing them, which meant that I had to say goodbye to women in the foreseeable future. Some thought that my commitment might mean I would not ever get married.

Later on, everything fit in perfectly when Djenny came into my life. She was a regular at church, yet I remained unmoved, and none of my thoughts were about her; I wanted to serve God and nothing else. However, things took a turn on one fateful Sunday, and I remember very clearly as I walked into the church and saw her there. As I was about to approach her, the Holy Spirit opened my heart and told me, "This is your wife." I had faith in Him and later addressed the same to Djenny – and she was a bit overjoyed, as she claimed that the Holy Spirit spoke the same to her that morning. Our paths crossed, not by random occurrence but rather by a divine blueprint that had been meticulously designed.

The Beginning of Our Shared Journey

On August 4, 2001, we were wed, marking the onset of a marriage grounded on faith. In Djenny's prior life, a modest woman lacked pride and worldly interests. I remember before getting married, I asked her if she wanted a grand wedding or if she wanted to spend that money on a house instead. Without a second thought, she replied that she preferred a house. Hence, we acquired our first home before the wedding. Three years later, we sold that home at an immense return. That was the start of our journey in real estate investment, a path God has blessed in remarkable ways.

Early Challenges and Growth

Marriage was an eye-opening journey and made me feel the need for more self-development. There is a difference between being a man and being a husband. It pains me to recall the day I got married – I walked in fully expecting to be 'the boss of the house' and that Djenny's role was to serve me. It is this kind of mentality that created tension between us. I always clamored to 'win an argument' rather than engage in an intelligent, insightful discussion to be heard and understood. Sometimes, we had our share of misunderstandings, miscommunications, and even moments of disrespect.

Everything changed when I studied Jesus and his relationship with the church. And I pondered, if Jesus loves the church and gives himself for her, I should also love, serve, and lead Djenny, my wife. As I sought the Holy Spirit's divine presence, I implored for a love that is unconditional and selfless. With His assistance, this relationship became less about us as a couple and more about Christ as the center's unique focal point of our relationship. It was an awakening for me. Instead of perceiving marriage as a status position, I saw it as an institution of loving service.

Becoming a Husband: A Journey of Growth and Learning

God created people but did not create them as husbands and wives. While man was formed with the potential to become a husband and woman with the potential to become a wife, these roles are not automatic. We do not all begin life as doctors, teachers, or mechanics; we acquire such knowledge while growing up. The same applies to a husband; it necessitates a process of learning, growth, and divine intervention. In His love and guidance, it is an actionable idea that should be embraced in life.

I wish I had done this earlier as a newlywed; I thought of it similarly. I assumed that a man becoming a husband was just something situational; the only work required was to get married. I did not realize that the role of a husband is not just about being a provider or a partner but about embodying Christlike love, protection, and service to my wife. Not being equipped with this knowledge prevented me from becoming a husband my wife needed to be with her.

The turning point came when I began studying Jesus's life and committing to follow His example. Jesus taught me what it meant to love sacrificially, protect selflessly, and serve faithfully. As I read the Word of God and allowed the Holy Spirit to transform my heart and mind, I began to see my role as a husband in a new light.

I learned that being a husband means:

- **Loving like Christ** means putting my wife's needs above mine and showing her unconditional love, even when it is complicated.

- **Protecting with care:** Not just physically, emotionally, and spiritually, ensuring she feels safe and secure in our relationship.
- **Providing faithfully:** Offering financial support, emotional presence, spiritual leadership, and unwavering encouragement.

This journey taught me that being a husband is a lifelong pursuit. Faithful husbands must be humble, ready to learn, and willing to submit to God's will as they grow each day.

Sadly, for many men, including me, it is a marriage without correctly comprehending the biblical concept of marriage. Instead, many men like me enter marriage with certain preconceived notions and assumptions. But God, in His grace, allows for growth to become the husbands He wants us to become.

In hindsight, I owe a debt of gratitude for how God has brought the necessary changes in me to be a more effective husband. My wife now is looking at the man who does not just talk about loving her but demonstrates it in actions: a man who cares for her as Christ loves the church. And that was not by my power but by the grace of God, through Jesus and the Holy Spirit.

Self-focused individuals may be surprised to learn that marriage is more than a relationship; it's a divine assignment. To achieve it, we need to depend on God, read his word, and let him shape us into the husbands and wives he made us to be.

The Journey of a Wife: The Role of Transformation

Just as God created man with the potential to become a husband, He created woman with the potential to become a wife. However, being born a woman does not automatically make someone a wife, any more than being born a man makes someone a husband. A woman must grow into a wife, learning from God, who designed her, and relying on His Word and Spirit to fulfill this sacred calling.

This process requires intentionality, humility, and a willingness to learn. Society often places expectations on women about what it means to be a wife, but true wisdom about this role comes from God, not the world. As God intended, a wife is more than a companion or homemaker; she is a partner, a nurturer, and a reflection of Christ's love and grace in the marriage.

When a woman embraces God's design for her as a wife, she learns to:

- **Love sacrificially:** Just as Christ loved the church, a wife learns to love her husband selflessly, supporting him in his strengths and weaknesses.
- **Nurture with grace:** She becomes a source of encouragement, peace, and care, building up her husband and home with wisdom and understanding.
- **Submit with strength:** Submission in God's design is not about weakness but about trusting God's order and walking in unity with her husband while exercising her God-given gifts and strengths.
- **Seek God's guidance:** A godly wife seeks God in prayer and relies on His wisdom to navigate challenges and grow in her role.

Just as several men go into marriage and cannot fully comprehend what it means to be a husband according to God's plan, the same applies to women. Some have to turn to sociological aspects or their anticipations, which creates barrenness, frustration, and a lack of fulfillment of needs in marriage relationships. But God, in His exceptional knowledge and love, has laid down in Scripture the instructions on how to be the bride that He intends every woman to be.

Becoming a wife is a changing process. When she learns about Jesus's life and teachings, she reveals the heart of a servant leader. And when she yields to the Holy Spirit, she has the insight and strength to support and build her marriage upon that rock.

A wife should strive for spiritual growth rather than perfectionism; it should be a journey to get closer to God and her husband. This move allows her to serve, love, and fulfill her communion with God as a wife even better.

Marriage is divinely ordained to both men and women and as an institution ordained by God, it must be continually worked on with love and patience. So, as husbands and wives operate in the light of God and His Word, they are part of Christ's life in that they stand in the place of love that He has for the Church as they perform their God-designed roles and praise Him.

Becoming a Father: A Journey Guided by God the Father

A man is both able to be a husband and a father. But it is important to note that not every man, or every husband, is meant to be a dad. Some men are single by choice or circumstance or have chosen such a course by divine design, wanting to remain childless, such as eunuchs or the infertile. There is a group for whom the call of God is to be Dads. But that is not how it works. It is modeling after

God the Father, which means it is a role that needs to be developed and requires hard work and sacrifice.

Fatherhood is not simply about biology or providing for a family; it is about reflecting the heart of God in the way a man leads, loves, and nurtures his children. God, the ultimate Father, provides the perfect example of what it means to be a father:

- **A Protector:** God shelters His children from harm as a shield against unseen and unseen dangers. A father learns to protect his children physically, emotionally, and spiritually, providing a safe environment for them to thrive.
- **A Provider:** Just as God supplies all our needs according to His riches, a father learns to provide not only material necessities but also emotional security, wisdom, and unconditional love.
- **A Teacher:** God teaches and disciplines His children out of love, guiding them in the right direction. A father must learn to instruct his children with patience and grace, imparting values and godly wisdom.
- **A Comforter:** God's presence brings peace and assurance to His children in times of trouble. A father learns to be a source of comfort, offering

compassion and encouragement during his children's struggles.

A man does not become a father the moment his child is born; fatherhood begins as he learns to walk in the character of God the Father. This process requires him to deepen his relationship with God, study His Word, and rely on the guidance of the Holy Spirit. Through prayer, humility, and a heart to serve, he becomes the kind of father who raises his children to know and love God.

For a man to become a godly father, he must first become a student of God the Father. He learns:

- **Patience:** Children require time and understanding as they grow, as God is patient with us in our shortcomings.
- **Sacrificial Love:** A father's love mirrors Christ's sacrifice, placing his children's needs above his own.
- **Forgiveness:** Just as God forgives us, a father learns to forgive and teach his children the power of grace.
- **Discipline with Love:** Discipline is not punishment but correction that leads to growth, reflecting God's loving discipline of His children.

I, too, did not fully understand the role of a father when I became one. Only by studying the life and love of God the Father did I grasp the depth of this responsibility. Through my journey of following Jesus, I learned to lead, protect, and nurture my children with the heart of a servant and the wisdom of God's Word.

I lacked a solid role model for marriage and father figures, so I was a little lost. But thanks to God, He made me the loving father that I wished to be in the past. Djenny and I have been able to raise a family based on love. This love and marriage that now binds us together is more potent than any other promise. As a father eager to grow with my four children, I have found it vital to adapt myself to the role of guidance, love, and motivation.

Fatherhood is a holy vocation that should be regarded with utmost seriousness and respect as an undertaking that calls for total dedication. It is about developing deeper and relying on God for empowerment and counsel for advancing posterity. A righteous father affects not only his children's destiny but also humanity's future, and his faith and love are handed over as a heritage for generations to come.

Being a Mother: A Journey of Obedience to God

There is a stewardship aspect to any relationship that God expects each wife to fulfill. The transition from wife to mother is similar to a woman who has to work to become a mother with God's assistance and direction. The complexity of God's purposes means that not all wives are mothers, although all wives have the potential to be mothers. Of course, God, in His infinite wisdom, has created some women to become mothers, but other women are made for different purposes. For those called to motherhood, it is not a position that comes fully formed. Instead, it is a sacred responsibility learned and cultivated by following God, who nurtures and cares for all His children.

Motherhood is far more than giving birth or raising children; it reflects God's nurturing, sacrificial, and unconditional love. God Himself provides the ultimate example of caring for, guiding, and growing others. In His image, a godly mother learns to embody qualities that mirror His character:

- **A Nurturer:** God tenderly nurtures His children, providing for their needs and comforting them in times of trouble. A mother learns to create a safe and loving environment where her children feel cherished and valued.

- **A Teacher:** Just as God instructs His children in righteousness, a mother teaches her children, imparting wisdom and biblical values that shape their character and faith.
- **A Protector:** Like God, who guards His children from harm, a mother learns to protect them from physical, emotional, and spiritual dangers, ensuring they grow in a safe and secure environment.
- **A Servant Leader:** God's love is sacrificial, putting the needs of His children first. A mother learns to prioritize her children's well-being with joy and grace, often at significant personal cost.

Motherhood involves embracing the virtues of self-denial, patience, and trust in God's guidance and grace. Since no one is naturally a mother, it consists of praying, going through trials, and wishing to imitate God. In winning through all losing episodes, a mother understands that she should not find her strength in herself but in God, who prepares her for the role.

Lessons for Becoming a Godly Mother

Before assuming her role as a mother, a woman must seek God's counsel to equip her for the task. This involves:

- **Sacrificial Love:** Just as Jesus laid down His life for us, so too does a mother love her children with Christ's love and devotion, which makes her sacrifice herself many times.
- **Patience:** Mothers must have the same patience God shows us in that we develop in Christ at our own pace. Children grow and develop independently, so the mother must exemplify patience.
- **Compassion:** The mother also learns to extend love to her children every time they stumble, for God's mercy is plentiful and new daily.
- **Discipline with Grace:** Discipline and Children are pruned with love to push kids towards maturity. A godly woman, however, balances this love so that she does not crush them. Instead, she builds their character.
- **Faithfulness in Prayer:** A mother's prayer is powerful. She consistently prays to stand in the gap for her children so they may be protected, wise, and spiritually grow.

My Journey of Learning

When I first became a father, I did not fully grasp the concept of Godly parenting. Similarly, my wife had to find ways and means of being a Godly mother when we had children. In that regard, we realized that motherhood, like fatherhood, is not an event but a progressive process. The effort along the journey is through the Holy Spirit to grow in the understanding of what it means to be a parent.

My wife became a worthy mother after devoting herself to God and His Word. She prayed, loved, and taught, reflecting God's motherly and gentle aspects. She sacrificed her career, dreams, and life to be the mother God wants for our children. I witnessed with my own eyes how God Himself prepares women for such an excellent position when they yield their hearts to Him.

A Divine Calling

Motherhood is one of God's most extraordinary callings, designed to nurture and raise children who will love and serve Him. A godly mother does more than care for her children—she plants seeds of faith, builds a foundation of love, and prepares her children to walk in the purpose God has for their lives.

Every woman can be a great image of God's love because she is tendered and loved by the Almighty, the One who is always active in her life. For those women who accept this role, motherhood is not just a role; it is a ministry and an example of God's grace, reflected through the ages.

Purpose and Timing in Marriage

Meeting Djenny taught me an invaluable lesson: Like Adam in the garden, focused on his God-given work, I concentrated on fulfilling God's purposes when He brought my wife into my life. God does not send a partner before He provides a mission and purpose. Before God gave Adam a wife, He gave him a purpose to fulfill, a mission to complete, and work to accomplish for His Kingdom. Adam's role was to reflect God's character and multiply His image on earth. When Eve entered his life, she found him already engaged in God-given work and joined him as his helper.

Likewise, if you dedicate yourself to God's work, He will provide the right partner at the right time to support His mission through your marriage. God saw that it was not good for Adam or me to be alone, so He brought our wives to walk beside us in fulfilling His purposes.

A Tribute to Djenny

As I write this book, Djenny and I celebrate 23 years of marriage. She is beautiful inside and out, a woman who loves God and others profoundly and lives with humility. She values our marriage and family and sacrifices much to nourish us spiritually and physically. Djenny is content serving behind the scenes, glorifying God in quiet humility.

I owe much of my professional journey to her. She saw my potential and encouraged me to pursue a master's in counseling psychology and, later, a doctorate, believing in my potential. Her unwavering support and partnership have been instrumental as we serve in ministry.

God's Grace in My Life

In hindsight, I remember how gracious God has been to me through Djenny. Although my past is quite rugged, God's grace gave me a pure wife. She always tells me, "You are the first man I know. You are the only one I will know with God's help." These words are genuinely challenging and motivational, increasing my resolve to love and serve her in a way that is faithful to her. With the guidance of God's Spirit, I am dedicated to serving and loving her wholeheartedly, now and forever.

Thank you, Djenny—for your faith, love, and unwavering partnership. I am eternally grateful.

CHAPTER 11:

A Call to Lead: Founding the Love Kingdom

The founding of Love Kingdom was not merely an act of establishing a place of worship; it was the manifestation of God's call on my life to create a community rooted in love, compassion, and genuine transformation. This chapter outlines my journey toward establishing this ministry, fueled by a deep conviction that serving others as Jesus did was the core of my calling. Through Love Kingdom, my hope has always been to build a spiritual home where people could learn about Jesus and experience His love in an authentic and life-changing way.

Vision: To be Like Jesus

When God placed in my heart to begin Love Kingdom, He beautifully placed the work to do in my heart. Love Kingdom was to be like Jesus, which I plan to regain. In this era of 'love only when it pleases me' or even 'where there is love, it is quite rare,' I have felt God to start a church nursing the characters of Jesus. A life modeled in selflessness, giving, sacrificial love, and love without condition became ours. The vision for Love Kingdom is not to be a collection of believers that come together for the sake of it but a place that is a center of revelation of Christ in the life and works of everyone who is a part of it.

All members are always amazed by this vision concept, for we virtually elaborate on it – it is the foundation of every ministry, every sermon, and every outreach event. We aim for individuals to witness Jesus as last through our worship, service, and relationships. I have always prayed that Love Kingdom would be a beacon, shining His love and drawing people to Him. Through acts of kindness, a warm welcome, or a message of hope, we strive to show people that Jesus is not a distant figure but a present and loving Savior.

The Mission: Loving God and Loving People

Our mission at Love Kingdom is built on two profound commandments that Jesus emphasized: *to love God with all our heart, soul, and mind and to love our neighbor as ourselves.* This mission goes beyond traditional ministry activities; it compels us to live out love in every interaction, both within and outside the church. Loving God is our foundation; our commitment to loving others flows out of that love. In general, it means bringing the mission into reality by Going to distinct locations within the community or outside of it. It means engaging with God's love for the lost, the lonely, and the hurting.

This love we have been discussing is unconditional love that replaces selfishness with sacrifice. Every brother, sister, disciple, and servant in Christ must work passionately towards this mission. This mission suggests we must step out of our comfort zones, engage people from every corner of society, and show through action that love is more significant than words. We are called to be Jesus' hands and feet, demonstrating that His love is accessible and that His grace is sufficient for everyone.

The Method: The Teachings of Jesus Christ

Jesus Christ is the cornerstone of our church structure and purpose. We emphasize His teachings in the Bible as our starting point, reference, and measure. The practices He taught are valid from centuries past and are properly applicable today. Every message, lesson, or discipleship class at Love Kingdom has one purpose: to show the people Jesus's love, life, and works.

What Jesus said, what He commanded, the parables He spoke in, and the examples He set the way we do all sorts of things. Whether it is about feeding people experiencing poverty or reaching out to the rejected, His life becomes a practice of how to treat other people. We desire to instill a spirit of humility, an attitude of servanthood, and engender patience, all discipleship virtues. Using sermons and direct ministry, we seek to teach our members who Christ is and thereby develop their faith.

The Empowerment: The Holy Spirit at Work

I believe that nothing of eternal value can be envisioned or accomplished without the enabling of the Holy Spirit. The Holy Spirit is the ministry's anchor of our strength, wisdom, and endurance. He encourages us during trials, reassures us in times of doubt, and nurtures us in times of outreach. As the founder of Love Kingdom, I trust the leading of the Spirit in all my decisions, conversations, and prayers.

Each time I see the Holy Spirit at work—whether in a moment of breakthrough, a life transformed, or a heart softened—I am reminded that He is the true leader of this ministry. My role is to listen, obey, and stay humble. The Spirit's work in my congregation and me enables us to accomplish what we could never do on our own. He empowers us to move mountains, heal broken hearts, and bring hope to those in despair.

Building Love Kingdom: A Journey of Faith

Setting up the Love Kingdom was not a walk in the park; huddles and battles were on the way. Every step required faith, perseverance, and a selfless attitude. I picked up early on that everyone is not called to lead a ministry out of personal ambition but instead out of obedience to God's command. At times, I was unsure whether the objective was within reach, and some parts were filled with insecurity, but each obstacle taught me valuable lessons in trust and surrender.

Gradually, we transformed from a small number of believers into a vibrant, purpose-driven body of people. Each person who joined us had varying gifts, stories, and struggles that complimented the beautiful fabric of Love Kingdom. We set out to present the world with an opportunity to meet Christ, get changed, and be molded to serve the kingdom of God.

Our walk of faith continues as we work to build a Love Kingdom where Jesus' arm and hand can be extended out. The journey of building the Love Kingdom has shown me that God provides exactly what we need when we need it. Sometimes, that provision is material, but often, it comes as renewed faith, resilience, and wisdom. This journey has been one of stepping out in faith, knowing that we walk not by sight but by trusting in His promises.

A Church Built on Love and Service

We strive to live according to Jesus Christ's ministry standards in the Kingdom of Love. We intend to serve without expecting to be served, heal the brokenhearted, and give hope to the hopeless. We are determined to be a church in which love is an act, a decision, and a way of living rather than just a word. We address spiritual and physical aspects through community service, outreach events, and support programs, demonstrating Christ's love.

We bind ourselves to many things, such as vision, mission, method, and empowerment, as we expand; that is to say, we never lose sight of where we are heading and place a lot of trust in God. We do not simply exist to add to the list of churches in the neighborhood; our reason for being here is to change peoples' lives and to let Christ's light shine out in the much-needed world. Each outreach, service, and all our relationships revolve around Christ's love, so we seek to embody love in all our endeavors.

An Encouragement to Future Leaders

In this chapter, I share the story of founding Love Kingdom as a testament to God's faithfulness and encouragement to those who feel called to step into leadership. Ministry is not easy, but it is rewarding to witness how God is changing lives; it requires sacrifice, humility, and complete reliance on God. I hope others will be inspired by the journey of Love Kingdom to trust God's timing, listen to His voice, and step boldly into His calling on their hearts.

As I stated earlier, Love Kingdom is a testament to what God can do through those willing to obey, love, and trust Him. With love, you can accomplish everything. All this ministry is an answer to his call, and with the Holy Spirit, I look forward to what he can do through us. My sincere effort is that Love Kingdom becomes the tool of God's love and grace, which brings people towards God and glorifies His name by changing lives with His power. During this journey, I have realized that the most significant vocation in this life is to be called to serve, love, and lead people to Jesus.

God called me to lead Love Kingdom, and my response has been to surrender fully to Him. This ministry is not about me. It is about His glory and His Kingdom, the People of God. As I look ahead, what He has done completely amazes me, and I am sure He will do even more as we continue with Love Kingdom.

CHAPTER 12:

From Counselor to Creator: A Journey of Talents

The story of my life is a testament to God's transformative power. Once an unwanted child, I grew into a man who would embrace not only the roles of pastor, husband, father, counselor, doctor, author, creator, and visionary. With the help of God, I have been able to receive a master's degree in counseling psychology, become a certified mental health professional, and achieve higher degrees of educational attainment in the form of an EdD. in community care and counseling, focusing on marriage and family counseling, and have further been able to shift my focus on other activities that I would never have thought would be possible. At every stage of this journey, starting from counseling and progressing to writing books and designing my sneakers that got featured in GQ magazine, one thing was consistent at every point, and it was God's hand that guided me to harness and showcase the potential that He had vested in me. This chapter unravels the journey of seeking a life devoted to these gifts and serves a purpose to glorify His faithfulness, goodness, and love.

Discovering My Talents

While I was a child, I never thought of the roads that God would walk me down. But every era in my life did unfold systematically, minus the entire image. When I took my first steps in the field of counseling, I found that the idea of helping people heal and find meaning was appealing to me. As a psychotherapist, I could serve, assist, and accompany people through their darkest moments. I became immersed in these activities. Over time, my practice of counseling became more than a job—it became my life's work and purpose.

Yet, God's vision for me extended beyond the office walls. He was opening doors for me to explore other gifts, some that had been quietly waiting to be discovered. During my journey as a counselor, I felt compelled to write—to share the insights and wisdom I had gained with a larger audience. It became increasingly evident that God intended to connect me to people transcending physical limitations, for He implanted the desire to write in me. I realized He never created anyone without several attributes within them that were all meant to bring honor and praise to Him.

Finding My Voice as an Author

There was a mountain to move from being a counselor to becoming an author, but I gladly turned to God, and at His instance, my feet began to move. My heart could express itself through the lessons I penned on faith, family, and personal development. I wrote to help, heal, and support others who had undergone similar challenges, hoping my suffering and surfaces could serve a purpose. Each book has made me realize that God has his ways, and as such, He can reach out and connect with people in diverse and unique ways.

My books became remarkable ways to spread the principles I preached through ministries and therapeutic science-based evidenced interventions during my counseling sessions, reaching people on different continents. With each book, I realized that God was enabling me to get others in a more profound, more personal way. My books became tools to share the principles I taught in counseling sessions, touching lives across miles and cultures.

On this day, as an author, I knew I would have to be more careful in disposing of my experiences since God's word is clear: He expects us to share the knowledge He has given us. Writing was no longer something I did for fun; it had become part of my work in the ministry, another way I could serve Him.

From Counseling to Creativity: Embracing New Expressions

Even though I had counseling and writing practice, which came quickly, God started to teach me more about creativity; this was a scenario I would have never imagined. To my surprise, the other was an intense yet exciting design interest. To me, design became one more articulation of aesthetics, emotion, or creativity. Specifically, however, I got interested in designing shoes and other items, such as T-shirts, which was exciting and surprisingly allowed me to express several aspects of my creativity.

It was pretty jaw-dropping when a sneaker I designed appeared on the GQ pages. It felt like a dream, but on the other hand, it helped me reflect on the power of the Lord and how far His plans can reach if we are willing to let Him use us and our gifts.

I first understood that God can communicate with people in any language or through any garment. The sneaker was more than just a product; it was a piece of my journey, representing how God had shaped me from an unlikely beginning into a creator who could bring beauty and innovation into the world.

Talents as Testimonies

Each skill—counseling, writing, or design—became a witness to God's goodness. I developed these skills and saw how the Lord used them to bless others. Through counseling, I saw people healed and set free from the bondage of sin. I wrote beyond what was for my family as an extension of faith to many who need hope. Through design, I started experiencing the thrill of creating to convey trust and resilience. Through ministry, I taught God's Word to draw others to Jesus and His Kingdom and help believers become disciples of Jesus and, in turn, make disciples of Jesus.

I have concluded that our talents are not just gifts but tools for ministry, a form of God's grace, and an opportunity to change someone. God can use the unlikeliest of gifts to complete his plan. Each talent was a separate way of reaching out to people and expressing his love through various forms.

Becoming a Husband and Father: God's Special Blessing Above All.

The journey of developing my talents was complemented by my growth in my most cherished roles: husband and father. God gave me the incredible gift of family—a loving wife and wonderful children who have been constant sources of support, joy, and inspiration. Becoming a husband and then a father expanded my heart in ways I could not have anticipated. These roles grounded me, teaching me patience, love, and selflessness on a profound level.

In my family, I see God's faithfulness every day. Whenever I am with my children, I remind myself that such an opportunity is brief and accentuates the importance of exemplifying Christ's love and establishing a legacy of faith for the next generation. The very first ministry is my family from all other activities. Everything I achieve stems from the strength and love that my family and I have, which God gives. As a father, I am driven to empower my children, lead them, and protect them so that they can learn and build on the talents they were born with and develop God-style imaginations.

Using Talents for God's Glory

In every stage, God has shown me that my talents are for His glory rather than me attaining my glory. He has given me these gifts not to achieve greatness but to help others, heal the broken, and share hope in Christ. My life's purpose is to serve Him, and in doing so, it is through ministry, counseling, writing, design, or anything that will positively impact the lives I meet. This particular mission is one of many, as I am constantly reminded that God does not call the qualified; he qualifies the called. Transitioning from an unwanted baby to being a pastor, a therapist, a doctor, a writer, and a creator, I am a testament to the fact that God's plans for us are indeed more extensive than we can fathom. Our gifts are in His Kingdom, whatever form they take, and it is through them that He reaches out to people and accomplishes His purposes on Earth.

This journey is a continuous reminder that God does not select the qualified; He qualifies the chosen. From an unwanted child to a pastor, counselor, author, and creator, I am living proof that God's plans for us are more extensive than we could ever imagine. Our gifts are in His kingdom, no matter how diverse or unexpected. They are the instruments through which He works, touching lives and advancing His purpose.

Moving Forward: A Life of Surrender and Service

Whenever I think about the progress of this journey as it unfolds, I yearn to know what more God will do with these abilities that I appear to have. I ask, pray, and hope to remain in tune with Him, ready to go to places I am uncomfortable and prepared to serve. Primarily, every skill I perform, every milestone I can reach, and every stage of this journey I merit is a remembrance of God's grace, mercy, and faithfulness.

It has always been, and it will always be. From counselor to creator, every stage of my life has been shaped by a desire to follow God's leading and a commitment to use my talents for His glory. My journey is a testament to what God can do when we surrender our lives and gifts to Him. I am grateful and committed to serving Him with everything He has placed in my hands. This is my story, calling, and purpose—to honor God with my talents, serve His people, and testify of His love through every avenue He opens before me.

CHAPTER 13:

Legacy and Love: Building a Lasting Impact

As I take a moment to reflect on my life, one of the most profound requests of my heart is to establish a legacy that will last for longer than my life, creating a difference in the several generations that will succeed me. A legacy does not solely speak of the milestones we achieve in this world but focuses on how we spend our time, talent, and resources and our impact on people through these things. This chapter explores how I strive to build a lasting impact through my life, ministry, and the Love Counseling Center. It is about using every opportunity to pass on the faith, wisdom, and love that have shaped me and to inspire others to embrace their God-given purpose.

The Power of Legacy

A legacy is often defined by the stories we leave behind—the ones we pass down to our children, our communities, and the generations that follow. It is the imprint of our lives that transcends time and circumstance. A lasting legacy is built through achievements, the values and principles we instill in others, how we lead, and the love we give.

When God spoke to me, I accepted his call with His help, and it dawned on me that my assignment was for today and the rest of my life. I had a powerful sense that I intended to be more than just a temporary channel for ministry and wanted to build something that would communicate Christ's message for generations to come. That vision has prompted me to invest in people, train successors, and set up structures enabling others to carry out their summons. I wish to create a chain reaction in all these endeavors, whereby a faith, love, and service thesis would be passed on to several ages.

Leading Others in Faith

The cornerstone of the legacy I hope to leave is rooted in leading others to Christ. From the founding of Love Kingdom to my work as a counselor and author, everything I do is intended to inspire others to live out their God-given purpose and follow Jesus with their whole hearts. Leadership, to me, is not about power or recognition—it is about service. Jesus was the ultimate servant-leader and set the example for us all.

I try to lead with humility, kindness, and a glorious sense of accountability to God and the people I serve. Jesus, as the Pastor, Counselor, and Mentor figure, has also enabled me to help people through their faith walk.

I am in a position to guide people as believers as they mature in a relationship with Christ through the Love Kingdom ministry, which I find to be very fulfilling. Every sermon, every prayer offered, and every service performed is a way to make deposits into the lives of those who have appointed me as their leader. My heart's prayer is to see these people develop in the faith and realize they can also lead others, thus generating a discipleship movement that spreads the Gospel of the Kingdom of God.

Establishing the Love Counseling Center

In addition to my ministry work, establishing the Love Counseling Center was one of the most significant steps I took in building a lasting impact. This center has become vital to my mission to help others discover healing, freedom, and purpose. The counseling center is more than just a place where people receive therapy—it's a sanctuary where individuals can come to experience God's transformative love, where marriages are restored, families are healed, and personal growth is nurtured.

In all these activities, the center reflects my vision and passion to serve people in totality—spirit, soul, and body. Over the years, I have seen countless lives transformed through our counseling services and the educational programs and workshops we host. The impact of the Love

Counseling Center extends beyond just the individuals who come through our doors—it touches families, communities, and even entire cities. Through this ministry, I can help people break free from the pain and dysfunction that hold them back, empowering them to live the whole, abundant life God intends.

Inspiring Others to Live Their Purpose

Speaking of purposes, one of the bright moments in my life has been seeing others go after their purpose. Whether Love Counseling Center, Love Kingdom, or personal mentor relations, I try to motivate people to be purposeful and manifest their gifts in the service of God and people. I have come to appreciate that true success is not measured by medals and titles won or the number of events I participated in but by how many people or things I helped to realize their destined purpose. I quite often try to reflect on what others can learn from my life story, especially those who feel the way I feel, are insecure or have very little sense of self-worth, do not think they have much to offer, and struggle to believe they can be a catalyst for change.

I have experienced things that most people would not be able to withstand, and as such, I can only hope that my testimony and how I live are enough to show anyone that regardless of their past and circumstances, God will always have a plan for them. It is a privilege to be a part of such a powerful testimony for God because anyone's background or situation does not limit him, and he proves this by using whoever he wants for His purpose.

Through mentoring and leadership development programs, I seek to cultivate an environment where people can discover their talents, strengths, and unique gifts. Whether through counseling, preaching, or community outreach, I help people recognize their potential and empower them to step into the fullness of what God has called them to be. There is no greater joy than seeing someone take the steps to live out their calling and begin to impact the world around them.

A Legacy of Love

The foundation of the legacy I desire to leave is love. Love is the greatest commandment Jesus gave us; it is the essence of everything I do. It is the driving force behind my ministry, counseling practice, marriage, and parenting. Love is the most potent force in the world, capable of healing wounds, mending relationships, and transforming hearts.

As I continue to build Love Kingdom, the Love Counseling Center, and other initiatives, I pray that my legacy will be saturated with love. I hope that when people look back on my life and ministry, they will remember that I loved God with all my heart and loved others selflessly. The lasting impact I wish to leave is not one of personal fame or recognition but of lives changed by the love of Christ.

The Future of My Legacy

As I look ahead, I trust that God will continue using me and my ministry to impact the world in ways I cannot imagine. My work still needs to be done, and I am excited for the opportunities He will provide to serve, lead, and inspire others. I hope that the legacy I leave will continue through the generations and that those who follow will continue to share the love of God with a world in desperate need of hope.

The legacy I seek to leave is not built on earthly accomplishments but on eternal impact. I pray that my life's story will be of faith, obedience, love, and service—one that points others to Christ and inspires them to live out their God-given purpose. Through the power of God's love, we can all leave a lasting legacy that will continue to echo through eternity.

Not what we leave behind materially, but the love we have shared and the lives we have touched truly define our legacy. And it is my deepest hope that when my time on this earth is done, I will have left a legacy of love that continues to inspire others to live out their God-given purpose for generations to come.

CHAPTER 14:

Your Story Matters: Embracing God's Purpose in You

As I close this book, I want to leave you with an invitation—a call to reflect on your story and the incredible journey God has guided you on. Your story matters. Every struggle you've faced, every joy you've experienced, every setback and triumph along the way has been part of the unique tapestry God has woven into your life. This chapter is not just an ending but an opportunity for a new beginning. It is a chance to recognize that your life has a purpose and that God has worked in you, even in ways you may not have fully understood or appreciated.

The Significance of Your Journey

We often feel our stories are too small, ordinary, or flawed to matter. We may look at others and think their journeys are more impactful, extraordinary, or meaningful. But I want to assure you today that your story is significant. No part of your journey has been wasted, and there are no moments of struggle that God has not used for His glory and your good.

God does not make mistakes, and He has perfectly crafted you for His purpose for your life. God is actively working in you, whether in a season of joy or hardship. Every experience, every person, and every moment in your life has been part of Their plan to bring you closer to the fullness of your calling.

Look at your life—where you have been, where you are, and where you are going—and recognize the incredible ways God has led, shaped, and refined you. Your journey is a testimony to His faithfulness, love, and transformative power. And it is a story that matters, not just for you, but for those around you and the world.

Embracing Your Struggles

People are bound to encounter obstacles when trying to achieve God's purpose. Along the way, there are hardships, challenges, painful experiences, and many more obscure memories. However, listen to me today. Those struggles are the ones that you should not let define you. Instead, it should be the other way around; those are the ones that should be embraced.

Whenever one is faced with struggles, it is God that one should call every single time. Struggles bring one closer to God. In a way, struggles are God's test of one's faith. Just as fire refines gold, our lives become filled with spiritual values as we grow older and mature. In these moments of trouble, we often discover our incredible strength.

These difficulties are part of your tale. God utilizes them to mold, instruct, and equip you for the forthcoming season in your life. God never abandons his storyline creation. When life seems unpredictable, His grace will always carry you through. Life can sometimes push you down to the point where you only need a little faith and a last push. You must realize he is with you in every situation: when the storms rage and the skies clear.

Such mountains are moved by faith. Have faith in God. Yes, such faith in God will make people and the world laugh. We all have a unique purpose in Him. Some already know what it is, and some are discovering it—that is all right. To achieve that, some believe being a force in the world helps; for some, it is a distraction.

To some people, this purpose may seem vain, but it keeps you going through rough patches. People need power and fame, but that does not mean we need to. The primary goal is to follow God's intentions, to take care of others, and to employ the gifts He has given you for better returns. Despite the least things, it is about making a lifetime difference because anything done in His name is never unimportant.

If you are feeling lost about your purpose, stay calm. Search for the Lord because He is the one who will produce a plan to achieve your purpose, and He will do it at the right time. Remember, purpose is often found not in what we do but in how we do it. Are you serving others? Are you loving those around you? Are you faithful to the gifts God has given you? Your purpose is knitted into the fabric of your everyday life.

Embracing Your Purpose

You must receive God's purpose and plan for your life, bring together your story and struggles, and then carry out the personalized plan God has for you. That means stepping into who He has made you to be in fullness. It does not mean you have to remain in a life beneath the plans God has crafted for you; instead, you can move forth by faith, confidence, and in the comfort of His plan.

Expressing God's purpose for you is complex and requires much submission. Seeking to accomplish your plans, goals, dreams, and desires are never appealed to. Instead, the whole point is that they have to be according to his will. It is all about surrendering and following God's words; that is a challenge, but it makes perfect sense. You live for a greater purpose, knowing that every dawn is another chance to praise God with an exemplary life.

Rest assured that God is your fortress, and you have purpose embedded within your heart for Him. You do not need to have every detail of the final plan figured out to make a move; you are only required to trust Him with the journey ahead, one day at a time. He will take you to places you have never fathomed before, which is a chance He grants you. Everything has been orchestrated to perfection, and every part of the plan you witness shall be a facet of God's work to enthrall you.

Living Out God's Design

To conclude, I challenge you to live out your story, to stop circling the point, and to be effective. Control whatever is pulling you away; do not let it control you. You must tend to that story; God's purpose is in you. Give it to people, surround them with the message, and let them drown in God's love, witnessing it firsthand.

If you suffer from self-doubt and confusion, find comfort in the fact that God is not done with you yet. That is not your endpoint; God is authoring your story with significant importance and aspiration. Let faith be the anchor for the next step you take. Fulfill God's purpose in your life, and rest assured that He will be there with you and use you to advance His Kingdom.

As you do, remember this: Your story matters. It matters to God, to those around you, and the world. Most importantly, your story matters because it is only embedded in you. Let everything you do display God's goodness, love, and faithfulness. Walk in His purpose and understand that He is with you every moment of your life.

May your life be a story that glorifies God and inspires others to embrace His purpose for them. Your story counts, and the world is waiting to hear it.

FINAL WORDS

As you come to the end of this book, I pray that our shared journey has inspired, challenged, and encouraged you. Life is a continuous unfolding of God's purpose for us, and every chapter we live is another step in His divine plan. It causes one to pause and contemplate life, for it is a journey. But let us keep this fact close to our hearts: Every birth is a testament to the Divine's ingenuity. Some are born as brides, mothers, fathers, husbands, wives, soldiers, and so forth. Yet, they all share something in common: they were made to fulfill a purpose – when one fails, the rest must be ready to disappoint the entire world. You were created for a purpose, and God has equipped you with everything necessary.

Do not give in even when every drop of your blood is trembling in fear. At times, it is necessary to kneel and pray even if you are the one who is boldly fearlessly standing there, and believe me, that takes nerves. Because I assure you, everything will fall into place with good faith and a little grace. Your values, morals, and everything you were ever raised with are the colors that will paint your canvas! Whether you are stepping into a new role as a husband, wife, father, mother, or leader—or simply striving to live as the person God created you to be—remember this truth: **You were made for a purpose, and God has equipped you with everything you need to fulfill it.**

I encourage you to accept the learning and maturing process in God. None of us are perfect the moment we start living. We become who we are supposed to be when we start praying to Him every day, emulating the life of Christ, and accepting the change the Holy Spirit introduces to us.

Always remember, there is nothing as powerful as love while you pursue God—the love of God for you, your love for God, and others. Love is the foundation of any role and relationship one may assume, and through love, we portray God in front of others.

Finally, know that you are not alone. God walks with you every step of the way. Lean on Him in your moments of doubt, trust Him in your seasons of growth, and rejoice with Him in your victories.

Thank you for letting me explain some episodes of my life and share my reflections. This book has encouraged you to live your vocation with courage, embrace your faith more fully, and experience the fullness of life He has created for you.

May God's favor be with you always, His protection be on you, and His power be in you so that you may shine in this world for His glory and honor.

May God bless you, guide you, and use you as a light in this world for His glory and honor.

With love and prayers,
Dr. Frantz Lamour

www.ingramcontent.com/pod-product-compliance
Lightning Source LLC
Chambersburg PA
CBHW062112080426
42734CB00012B/2834